The WORD Diet

Eva,
The best to you always
Theresa Byrd Smith

Theresa Byrd-Smith

WESTBOW
PRESS®
A DIVISION OF THOMAS NELSON
& ZONDERVAN

Unless otherwise indicated, all Scripture quotations are taken from the Holy Bible, New Living Translation, copyright © 1996, 2004, 2007 by Tyndale House Foundation. Used by permission of Tyndale House Publishers, Inc., Carol Stream, Illinois 60188. All rights reserved.

Scripture taken from the Holy Bible, NEW INTERNATIONAL VERSION®. Copyright © 1973, 1978, 1984, 2011 by Biblica, Inc. All rights reserved worldwide. Used by permission. NEW INTERNATIONAL VERSION® and NIV® are registered trademarks of Biblica, Inc. Use of either trademark for the offering of goods or services requires the prior written consent of Biblica US, Inc.

Scripture taken from the King James Version of the Bible.

All Scripture quotations in this publications are from The Message. Copyright © by Eugene H. Peterson 1993, 1994, 1995, 1996, 2000, 2001, 2002. Used by permission of NavPress Publishing Group.

License Agreement for Bible Texts World Bible Translation Center Last Updated: July 27, 2001 Copyright © 2001 by World Bible Translation Center All rights reserved.

WestBow Press books may be ordered through booksellers or by contacting:

WestBow Press
A Division of Thomas Nelson & Zondervan
1663 Liberty Drive
Bloomington, IN 47403
www.westbowpress.com
1 (866) 928-1240

ISBN: 978-1-5127-7478-8 (sc)
ISBN: 978-1-5127-7479-5 (hc)
ISBN: 978-1-5127-7477-1 (e)

Library of Congress Control Number: 2017901833

Print information available on the last page.

WestBow Press rev. date: 02/27/2017

CONTENTS

ACKNOWLEDGMENTS

I thank—

James, my husband. Thank you for letting me be me, accepting me just as I am, and faithfully loving and supporting my many pursuits. I love you deeply, James.

My loving family. Julius, Esther, Julia, and Rita Sharon, the Byrd's of Brier. Thank you, Mama and Daddy, for the love and life you provided me. "Direct your children onto the right path, and when they are older, they will not leave it" (Proverbs 22:6). Each of you played a distinct role in shaping my ever-evolving self.

My pastor, Dr. Bill Winston, who first alerted me to the importance of my words. Your profound leadership and teachings have changed my life forever. Thank you, Pastor!

Pastor Chris Oyakhilome, Dr. David Oyedepo, Kenneth M. and Gloria Copeland, Dr. Myles Munroe, and Andrew Wommack are among the several spiritual greats who provide consistent gleanings for my spiritual diet.

Kimberly Williams, my editor extraordinaire. You heard my heart and helped me put it into words. I believe God put us together as a team. I could not have done it without you. Thank you ever so much.

Loretta Baker-Jackson, my spiritual sister. Thank you for your friendship and love and for passing on your constant encouragement and faith so I could complete this work.

Many other encouragers whose faith in me kept me on the path to completion directly and indirectly. Though you may be unaware of your part, I have not forgotten your words and prayers.

Thank you!

Rita Sharon Byrd-Williams, my sister, you are engraved in my heart. This one's for you, Rita!

Millions of Americans seem to be burdened with excess weight. We point our fingers—accusingly—at what we eat, our lack of exercise, food portions, food availability, and a whole lot more. Most assuredly, all the above are contributing factors and major players in the weight-gain game. Those reasons are not to be discounted, but *The Word Diet* compels us to look at a seldom—if ever—considered source of weight: our words!

Inside, you will learn

- words carry weight
- the importance of our words
- the impact our words have on our lives

Inside, you are provided with Word weight-loss tools.

- the Word diary
- *The Word Diet* Exchange System
- free words
- anointed activities
- Word recipes that use the Word of God as the main ingredient

The takeaways are

- a loss of word weight that may be hindering you from realizing your God-given potential
- changed words that equal a changed life

You're invited to

- Step into *The Word Diet* kitchen and learn to "Cook with the Book."

Need to lose weight? Have traditional diets failed you? Want to take a different path to weight loss? Want some recipes to help you lose weight *and* keep it off? Discover *The Word Diet*, a diet that beckons you to consider what comes *out* of your mouth as opposed to what goes *in* it when trying to lose weight.

The Word Diet invites you to examine weight, weight gain, weight loss, and dieting through an entirely new mind-set. Discover what could be the real culprit behind the excessive weight you carry.

Dieting, by nature, can be drudgery. Even the word *diet* elicits an adverse reaction for many of us because we tend to associate that term with restrictions or regulations: food deprivation, limitations, and rules! Living in a land of excess, we don't particularly care for restrictions of any sort. We love to push the limit. The very thought of being *restricted* from eating the foods we want in the amount we want and when we want is unthinkable! The thought of dieting can actually prompt our imaginations to create stimuli that make us hungry! Our mouths begin to salivate as we imagine all the foods we will miss by limiting our intake or removing our favorite foods from our daily regimen.

Similarly, some people feel the same about words; they find it unimaginable not to say what they want to say when and where and to whom they want to say it. Understandably, making the commitment to stick with a diet can be difficult. Let's face it—dieting of any kind requires discipline.

The Word Diet is designed to help you lose the weight of words that are preventing you from reaching your God-given potential and becoming the person that God designed you to be. Our ability to use words as a means of communication is a powerful, God-given gift that only human beings possess.

We will take a look at the power of words formed in our minds, believed in our hearts, and spoken from our mouths as well as their relationship to the excessive weight: the burdens, pressures, and loads so many carry.

The Word Diet contains three integral components: Power Principles, Power Tools, and Power Recipes, all of which will teach, provide, and supply the necessary ingredients for you to become your best you. If you have ever uttered the words "I need to lose some weight," this book is for you!

Are you ready? Let's get started! Everything you need is in God's Word, so let's learn to "Cook with the Book!"

Read on!

PART I

The Word Diet Power Principles

CHAPTER 1

What Is *The Word Diet?*

The Word Diet is a spiritual diet that places God's life-bearing Word at the forefront of what comes out of our mouths. The spiritual aspect of *The Word Diet* does more than monitor what we take in through regular dietary consumption; it regulates, reestablishes order, and realigns our hearts by setting up a parameter of healthy word options that edify the mind, body, soul, and spirit.

Words can be burdensome and carry enormous weight. The words we speak are authentic indicators of the heavy loads we carry on the inside. The word *weight* refers to something heavy; it means to hold or press down, or it can refer to a burden or pressure.[1] When we speak in a way that's self-contained, limiting our words to ourselves, our lives, or each other, the weight of those words can bear down on us, pulling us into an abyss of major depression.

The Word Diet is designed to teach you to observe and examine what you say and what you believe when analyzing the source of unwanted, excessive heaviness. You will learn to lose the weight of words that hinder you from realizing God's good plans for you. You will learn to speak God's life-bearing, non-burdensome Word.

Many people attribute excess weight to the overconsumption of food, hence, the preponderance of diets and dieters. Consumption is certainly a contributing factor, but it is not the whole truth. Did you know that words can duplicate the feeling of weightiness as an actual physical burden? We've all heard, "Sticks and stones may break my bones but words will never

---

[1] "weight," Merriam Webster.com, http://www.merriam-webster.com.

hurt me." The fact is that words can and do hurt! Words carry influence, power, and consequence. Mishandling words can stop us from walking in our divine endowment. Whether spoken by us or by others, ill-fated words become deeply ingrained in our inner selves.

Components of *The Word Diet*

Food Choices

The food of choice is the Word of God. Regular diets provide natural foods for the body, but *The Word Diet* provides spiritual food for the soul, "soul food." God's Word provides a level of spiritual nourishment that is often underrated, but it is integral to keeping excess word weight off: "People do not live by bread alone, but by every word that comes from the mouth of God" (Matthew 4:4).

Recipes

Typical diets furnish food recipes. The recipes in *The Word Diet*, however, consist of spiritual declarations, confessions, and confirmations: "Thou shalt also decree a thing, and it shall be established unto thee: and the light shall shine upon thy ways" (Job 22:28 NKJV).

Word Exchange Plan

Just as natural diets exchange calorie-laden foods for nonfattening, healthy foods, *The Word Diet* exchanges negatively laden, self-contained words for God's Word: "All scripture is given by inspiration of God, and is profitable for doctrine, for reproof, for correction, for instruction in righteousness" (2 Timothy 3:16 NKJV).

Word Diary

Dieters often keep a food diary, tracking calories and food consumed. Likewise, word dieters are encouraged to use a Word diary (part II). "Then the Lord said to Moses, Write down all these instructions, for they represent the terms of the covenant I am making with you and with Israel" (Exodus 34:27).

Free Words

Typical diets provide negative-calorie foods that can be eaten freely without weight gain. *The Word Diet* provides God's non-condemning words that can be spoken freely with no added heft.

Activity Guidelines

The Word Diet recommends a combination of physical and spiritual activities (part II).

One-on-One Support

Typical diets may provide support in the way of forums, FAQs, call-ins, live chats, blogs, and so on. *The Word Diet* provides 24/7 help in the form of the living God: "I will answer them before they even call to me. While they are still talking about their needs, I will go ahead and answer their prayers" (Isaiah 65:24).

Guarantee

The Word of God provides God's personal assurance. He is the ultimate yes! "It is the same with my Word. I send it out, and it always produces fruit. It will accomplish all I want it to, and it will prosper everywhere I send it" (Isaiah 55:11).

Results May Vary

As with any diet, individual results vary due to a person's variations in application, faith, and consistency. However, God never varies; His Word does not change, and He cannot lie: "God is not a man, so he does not lie. He is not human, so he does not change his mind. Has he ever spoken and failed to act? Has he ever promised and not carried it through?" (Numbers 23:19).

Why *The Word Diet?*

In the United States, food is a central theme of life. In fact, it is a significant part of many gatherings—familial, business, and social. We spend a great deal of time contemplating and talking about food. We ask ourselves, *"What will I eat for breakfast?"* *"What am I going to have for lunch?" "What's for dinner?"* We ask others, "Where shall we eat out?" "What's on the menu today?" "Let's try this new restaurant!" "I have a new recipe." "I need to make a grocery list." "I must stop at the grocery store on my way home."

Likewise, much of the world today is concerned about food: Is there enough? Is it safe? Is it healthy? Certain populations in some parts of the world are starving while other populations, particularly in America, fight the battle of the bulge. In 2015, the Centers for Disease Control and Prevention reported, "more than one-third of American adults were overweight or obese"[2]

With the exception of trained chefs and other food connoisseurs with sophisticated palates, few of us can determine the ingredients in the food we consume. Only fairly recently have we begun to question food ingredients. Perhaps it is because so many of us no longer do our own cooking. Sitting at the dining table to share a family meal is not as common today as it once was; our schedules may not even permit us to share meals. The daily necessity of eating has become a secondary activity in many households. We often eat on the run, grabbing a bit of food as we dash out the door and not paying much attention to what we gobble up.

American eating habits have worsened,[3] our health is declining, and America is bulging. We are now realizing that there is a "heavy" price to pay for sloppy eating. Consequently, dieting in America has become a national pastime. Millions of Americans are dieting each year and spending billions on weight-loss products. Wikipedia reveals that there are vegetarian diets, semi-vegetarian diets, weight-control diets, low-calorie and very low-calorie diets, low-fat diets, crash diets, detox diets, medical diets, and other miscellaneous diets that fall under this list.[4]

A typical diet can help people lose weight, but most people tend to regain some—or even all—of those lost pounds. *The Word Diet*, by contrast, teaches you to permanently lose the bulk of word weight by shedding pounds of unhealthy words, and it carries an earnest expectation of not regaining the unwanted heaviness.

---

[2] "adult obesity facts," www.cdc.gov/obesity/data/adult.html.
[3] Sharpe.
[4] "list of diets," Wikipedia.com, https://en.wikipedia.org/wiki/List_of_diets.

The Word Diet Is Simple

At times when we diet, we simply need to throw out unhealthy foods. In this instance, the unhealthy items are perishable words. In *The Word Diet*, the concentration is placed on the words we speak as opposed to the foods we eat. The premise of *The Word Diet* can be summed up with this question: What are *you* saying? Here, we learn that like food, words can be healthy as well as unhealthy. Words can be excessive, and just like certain foods, some should be restricted.

The Word Diet calls into action the elimination of unhealthy words, utilizing instead words that edify, nourish, and build up. This dine-in or carry-out menu equips you with verbal alternatives that are more suitable to your spiritual palate and allow you to make healthier choices by exchanging negative words for God's life-bearing Word.

Much as a regular diet can, a diet of healthy words can affect our bodies, our minds, and our spirits as well as influence how we live. The weight-loss principles in *The Word Diet* are applicable to nearly any area of life.

The Word Diet Is Portable

The Word Diet requires that you feast on the Word of God. One of the benefits of consuming God's manna is that you can easily transport this meal everywhere you go. This is a spiritually edible dish that can be packaged for takeout, allowing you to carry it in your pocket, purse, briefcase, or hands—but most important, in your heart. God's sustenance is shelf-stable, never spoils, and will not lose its power.

The Word Diet consists of specific prepared meals from the Word of God. The recipes are delicious to the mind, tasty to the spirit, satisfying to the soul, and edifying to the body. Just as your natural person needs natural food for sustenance, you are encouraged to nourish your spiritual person with spiritual food by "chewing cud"—meditating the Word of God daily: "Study this Book of Instruction continually. Meditate on it day and night" (Joshua 1:8). Snacking is encouraged! Best of all, there is no need to call ahead for a reservation to dine, as God's Word is a ready Word.

Each recipe will whet and excite your spiritual taste buds and delight your soul's palate. As with any recipe, feel free to combine the contents to create a uniquely satisfying meal suitable to your tastes. There will surely be a tasty morsel that will hit the spot regardless of where you are in your faith walk. What are you hungry for?

The Word Diet provides multiple menu options: breakfast, lunch, dinner, appetizers, main dishes, desserts, and snacks. The recipes are adaptable to any meal occasion. You may desire an appetizer, a customarily light, bite-sized Word appropriate for the new believer. On the other hand, various confessions may be suitable for an entrée, a somewhat heavier spiritual meal uniquely pertinent to the "meat" eater. Whatever your preference, the choice is yours.

The Word Diet recipes, though delicious, add no extra poundage. This concept is a new way to prepare and consume a meal—a spiritual meal— calorie free! When you stick to this diet, you will develop a cultivated palate, a discerning taste for spiritual nourishment from the Word of God. The faithful follower of *The Word Diet* will shed pounds of words that carry worry, fear, doubt, and defeat subsequently resulting in a new person. As with most diets, *The Word Diet* must be adhered to daily to see lasting results.

If you hunger and have an appetite for God and His Word, *The Word Diet* promises to satisfy your cravings. Now that the shopping has been done and items have been acquired to prepare a hearty meal; all that is left for you to do is simply *stir* in prayer, *fold* in faith, *pour* in patience, *garnish* with gratitude, *sprinkle* with diligence, and *coat* with perseverance.

If you're ready to lose some word weight, I'm headed to *The Word Diet* kitchen. Follow me and learn to "Cook with the Book."

CHAPTER 2

What's the Big Deal about Words?

"The tongue can bring death or life; those who love to talk will reap the consequences" (Proverbs 18:21). That's an audacious statement! Multitudes of scripture address the importance of our words. If none of the others gets our attention, Proverbs 18:21 should. This verse is practically waving a red flag right before our eyes, and yet we continue to miss its significance. Words are plentiful, spoken so naturally by humanity that we hardly consider that words invoke such power: the power of *life* and the power of *death*. Who knew? Words are a big deal because they can set events in motion, cause things to be that once were not: "Then God said, 'Let there be light,' and there was light" (Genesis 1:3).

The spoken word is creative! If you have faith and doubt not, you can have what you say (see Mark 11:23). The foundation of *The Word Diet* is built on that verse. Let's examine further evidence of the power of words.

Starting in the garden, God created the world by speaking. From biblical accounts, we know the earth was void, without form, empty. Then, "God said" ... "and He said" ... "and He said" ten times in the first few verses of Genesis 1. God spoke this world into existence; He "said," and it was so!

God spoke until there was light, land, vegetation, waters, beasts, and fowl.

> The Lord merely spoke, and the heavens were created.
> He breathed the word, and all the stars were born. He
> assigned the sea its boundaries and locked the oceans in

vast reservoirs. Let the whole world fear the Lord, and let everyone stand in awe of him. For when he spoke, the world began! It appeared at his command. (Psalm 33:6–9)

Don't miss this: God created something from nothing using only the words He spoke. No mass production or assembly line required; just God, just words.

Stern warnings are given and fierce consequences await those with lying, deceitful, slanderous, hypocritical, envious, or malicious words. Our words serve as witnesses to our character. No word is idle, all have consequences. God's Word admonishes us not to talk in a foul, abusive, or unwholesome manner as words can free us or sentence us: "The words you say will either acquit you or condemn you" (Matthew 12:37). In the Bible, the tongue is described as wicked, untamable, and capable of corrupting the whole body. This is not just limited to our individual physical bodies but is inclusive of conglomerates such as the whole church.

Knowing when to speak and when to keep silent keeps us out of trouble. We are to speak guardedly. The tongue witnesses against anyone feigning a relationship with God; start talking and your identity will be revealed. "Some people make cutting remarks, but the words of the wise bring healing" (Proverbs 12:18). Words are mighty! We need to give stringent attention to the words we speak. Our words can cause or prevent woes.

The unlimited power of language has not been overlooked by God.

Look! He said. The people are united, and they all speak the same language. After this, nothing they set out to do will be impossible for them! Come, let's go down and confuse the people with different languages. Then they won't be able to understand each other. (Genesis 11:6–7)

In that way, the LORD scattered them all over the world, and they stopped building the city. (Genesis 11:8)

The wickedness of the human heart combined with the creative power of the same language would have given the people the ability to accomplish anything they decided to do. Confusion of language served to hinder their goals; they could no longer readily communicate with one another. A common language—words—would have permitted the people to carry out their own desires in spite of God's wishes.

What are God's wishes for believers? Jeremiah 29:11 tells us that God plans only good things for His children: "For I know the plans I have for you, says the Lord. They are plans for good and not for disaster, to give you a future and a hope." God says in 3 John 1:2 that He wishes us to prosper and be in good health. If God's plans for us are good—for us to be healthy in body and strong in spirit— but things in reality are not turning out like that, we need to ask ourselves, *what happened? Are we following God's plans?*

We can deduce from these and other scriptures that something happens between God's "good plans" for us and the actuality of our life experiences. Since God is never wrong and cannot lie, we are forced to examine ourselves. A study of the scriptures confirms that much of what happens to us has to do with what comes out of our mouths. What are we confessing? What are we thinking? What do we really believe? God has His plans for us, but our mouths can thwart those plans.

God has allowed us certain freedoms; one of them is choice, and it is evident that our spoken words convey these choices. It is very common, especially after a devastation, to hear, "Why did God allow this to happen?" You may not like this, but it is not meant critically. It is convenient for us to hold God responsible and walk away innocently. Perhaps the more appropriate questions might be "What has been spoken?" or "What has been believed?" That is not to say we deliberately choose devastation, but we must realize the Word of God says we have an enemy, Satan. Could he be lurking in our words on the alert for the opportunity to devour us? Absolutely! Who said, "What you don't know won't hurt you"? Not only can it hurt you, it can kill you. Be mindful: Hosea 4:6 says, "My people are being destroyed because they don't know me." Let's look further and gather additional knowledge about the power of words: "You don't have enough **faith**, Jesus told them. I tell you the truth, if you had faith even as small as a mustard seed, you could **say** to this mountain, Move from here to there, and it would move. Nothing would be impossible" (Matthew 17:20).

God made this declaration on more than one occasion (see Luke 17:6) All God's Word is profitable, but when He says it more than once, amplify it: "I tell you the truth, you can **say** to this mountain, May you be lifted up and thrown into the sea, and **it will happen**. But you must really **believe** it will happen and **have no doubt** in your heart" (Mark 11:23). Notice how the key words highlighted in the previous scriptures make up a formula.

Say + Believe + Have no doubt = It will happen!

Did you also notice that each emphasized word requires an action to reach the appropriate solution or yield a favorable outcome? Action is always a necessary component of faith.

The Works of the Tongue

The tongue is compelling; it is such a small yet mighty member. Remarks can be cutting, but the wise speak prudently. The tongue is namby-pamby, wishy-washy, and indeterminate. How is it that we use the same tongue to profess love one minute and replace it with poison the next? "Blessing and cursing come pouring out of the same mouth. Surely, my brothers and sisters, this is not right!" (James 3:10). Our words identify what we truly believe; they reveal what is in the heart, and who we are—our true character.

WORKS OF THE TONGUE	SCRIPTURAL REFERENCE
Lying Tongue	(Pro. 25:18) (Joh. 8:44) (Pro. 6:17) (Rev. 21:8)
Flattering Tongue	(Psa. 5:9)
Swift Tongue	(Pro. 18:13) (Jam. 1:19)
Proud Tongue	(Psa. 12:3-4) (Pro. 8:13b) (Pro. 16:15)
Piercing Tongue	(Pro. 12:18) (Col. 4:6)
Cursing Tongue	(Rom. 3:13-14)
Gossiping Tongue	(Pro. 18:8)
Overworked Tongue	(Ecc. 5:3)
Backstabbing Tongue	(Rom. 1:30)

Words Carry Life

Here's an experiment: hold your hand close to your mouth with palm facing forward and speak. Did you notice a warmth coming from your mouth? That warm breath you feel while forming the words as you speak is the very breath that carries life.

Without breath, we'd not be able to speak and we couldn't live! We are one with our breath and therefore one with our words. Suffice it to say that words carry life.

Words Are Potent

"When the breath, or spirit, of a man leaves, that man dies. The Spirit alone gives eternal life. Human effort accomplishes nothing. And the very words I have spoken to you are spirit and life" (John 6:63).

Words Are Paramount

The Word of God teaches us that our words drive the direction of our lives. Words can energize, inspire, challenge, change, control, persuade, engage, evoke, clarify, explain, mislead, and confirm.[5] Words can also create images, affect emotions, influence opinions, and shape perspectives. Words can alter our lives. Words like their consequences can be positive or negative.

Positive words create supportive stereotypes, while negative words create detrimental stereotypes. Just as words have power to tear down, they can also build up. We, God's people, have a job to do: "build up others" (1 Thessalonians 1:11). We are to be mature Christians not given to every whim that comes along. We are admonished to walk in love proclaiming the truth of God's Word in love not in judgment.

Let our words convey *agape*, the highest form of love; the love God has for us. A kind word or a simple acknowledgment that says "I see you" or "I appreciate you" adds value to an individual. Words have the ability to encourage and affirm. Consider how good you feel when well-placed words are spoken to you; discouragement, defeat, and even anger flee. Words have the ability to turn gloom into glee.

The Bible compares kind words to gold (Proverbs 12:25). It admonishes us to encourage and strengthen one another. This can be done by word or deed. For example, a salesperson at a store I often frequent invariably

---

[5] Tennyson.

scowled and tended to be curt. I did my best to avoid the checkout line she handled until one day, I sincerely admired her beautifully manicured nails. She looked up at me with a warm thank you. Since that day, her attitude toward me has changed. She now makes eye contact and greets me with a smile.

I make a practice of always greeting clerks with a smile and by asking, "How are you today?" before transacting my business. In essence, I'm saying, "I see you. You are valuable." Though it often startles them, I am acknowledging that someone in the horde of people they serve appreciates them. Try it! It could improve your service, but most important, it will brighten their day.

Another example of the power of words occurred recently when a former grade school student, now an adult, contacted me through a social networking site. I had not heard from her since her years in grade school. We met for lunch, and the meeting was phenomenal for both of us. She contacted me to tell me how much my words of encouragement had meant to her as a student such a long time ago, yet she remembered! I was her school principal at the time, and she never forgot our conversations in my office. She thanked me profusely, but I had no idea she was carrying those words in her heart.

Similar scenarios have happened to me involving former students, parents, and employees. God had blessed me with work in a profession in which I had the privilege of speaking into the lives of others. I am thankful that my words never abused that privilege.

CHAPTER 3

How Did I Get So Fat?

Do you feel heavy or weighted down and wonder when, where, or how that happened? This excess "weight" might not be associated with caloric intake or physical weight gain. Instead, the weight of unsavory words could be the culprit that is making you feel heavy and bogged down. Many of us are unaware that we have picked up any word weight. It is not as easily detected as physical pounds.

You may have been journeying down this road of heaviness since childhood. Chances are you have likely not been introduced to the concept of word weight until you picked up this book. Even so, you should be aware that negative or idle words spoken by us, to us, and about us can produce a perception of weightiness as though we were carrying the world on our shoulders. Having worked with youngsters in school settings for many years, I have observed a few of the sources of word-weight gain firsthand.

Self-Comparison

Self-comparison is a favorite sport of children. This unhealthy practice can begin inside the home through sibling rivalry and may continue in the classroom. It can spill into our work environments later. The cycle can be relentless throughout adulthood as many people permit the success of others to become their benchmarks of success. Escaping comparisons is not easy especially for young people growing up in a celebrity-crazed society that pits us against one another in a world of never-ending competition.

Young people in particular are affected by self-comparisons as they contend with what they believe are their inadequacies. Some have caused injury to themselves to look or be like someone else. We may look at another and think we are not as attractive, smart, wealthy, or accomplished simply because we do not perceive the same qualities in ourselves or have comparable materials as others. Though self-comparisons happen frequently and in various places, the Bible warns us not to compare ourselves to others: "You must not covet ... anything else that belongs to your neighbor" (Exodus 20:17).

Comparing ourselves to others is just the beginning of word-weight troubles. We may pick up the weight of inferiority, self-doubt, and unworthiness by engaging in self-comparison. In extreme cases, we begin to self-destruct, calling ourselves stupid, disorganized, fat, ugly, and even worthless. We begin to burden ourselves with the weight of our words. Each of us has different strengths. There will always be others who can perform certain tasks better than we can or have more possessions than we do.

Likewise, there will always be something we can do better than others, and we may possess something tangible or intangible that another wishes he or she had. Comparisons keep us craving everything we see and being prideful of our achievements and possessions. Comparisons are destructive, stressful, and weighty.

Cultural Mores

The dominant culture in a society decides what is and is not acceptable. Often, those who do not share the established ways feel locked out. Instances of continual unflattering verbal and written exchanges, unattractive portrayals by the media, and most important, words, contribute to negative attitudes and opinions. Over time, these attitudes and opinions when expressed can result in word weight.

Failure to live up to parental expectations often result in crushed feelings and stinging and defeating words. Low expectations voiced by authority figures such as schoolteachers, supervisors, etc., can all add word weight.

Taunting, Teasing, and Bullying

In my days as a school principal, I have seen my share of children taunted to tears with unflattering names and nicknames inflicted on them based on physical traits such as weight in particular, height, skin color, hair, eyes, etc. Teasing because of poor eyesight and the need to wear glasses or tattered clothing and so many trivialities can be sources of word weight picked up and carried through school days. Schoolchildren specifically struggle with hurtful and heavy word weight that is bullying. Such antics can leave scarring that lasts a lifetime. This weight is often too heavy for an adult to bear; can you imagine how easily a child will break down under such a heavy load?

Judgments, Disapprovals, and Rejection

Drawing again on my pedagogical experiences, I have witnessed children pick up word weight because of recurring academic failure. Frequent verbal judgment and rejection, especially those involving authority figures (parents, teachers) may also contribute to word-weight gain. The repeated dismissals and verbalized opinions of others brought on by innumerable experiences could be another source of word-weight gain.

Hostile Environments

Home environments, school environments, work environments, and the rhetorical experiences encountered in these arenas can potentially add word weight. These examples could be a source of the weight we pack on due to what has come out of our mouths or the mouths of others while we were in those places. *The Word Diet* aims to correct the ill-fated course of our words. Our mouths tend to speak what our thoughts have meditated on. Before we can correct our mouths, we need to correct our thoughts; one is dependent on the other.

Though Christians quickly concede that God requires us to hold our tongues, have compassion, and stay away from wicked and abusive talk, have we given much thought to what we are thinking? We talk to ourselves via our thoughts; we engage in an incessant inner chatter of self-talk mostly unaware of how it affects us. We've all witnessed another's lips moving and yet there is no one else in the vicinity. Chances are that person was talking to himself or herself—reasoning, thinking, memorizing, etc. We all do that. Our thoughts can be very demeaning, intrusive, or get-in-your-face loud until they suck the life out of us and stop us in our tracks from fully realizing our godly gifts. Unfavorable thoughts can evoke fear and doubt. Negative thoughts are ceaseless and can result in a type of paralysis, an inability to move forward. I often hear it said, "I can't stop thinking about it" and "I can't help what I think about."

How do we go about controlling our thoughts? It starts with a renewal of the mind, a common phrase in church circles. A renewal of the mind according to God's Word means changing the way you think. "Don't copy the behavior and customs of this world, but let God transform you into a new person by changing the way you think. Then you will learn to know God's will for you, which is good and pleasing and perfect" (Romans 12:2).

To renew involves an exchange, a trade. You trade an old object for a new object. For example, I recently renewed my driver's license. I went to the Department of Motor Vehicles, turned in my old license, and received a new one. This process involved a trade, yielding something I once possessed in exchange for something new.

Renewal of the mind works much the same. You have a mind that houses old thoughts from your previous way of life, from before you accepted Jesus as Savior and Lord. Those old thoughts that said you were sick, tired, broke, depressed, stupid, fat, ugly, lazy, or any other ungodly epithet have expired! You are now washed with the water of the Word. The old way of doing, thinking, and being is replaced by a new way—God's way—of doing, thinking, and being. This constitutes a renewal of the mind.

"We use God's mighty weapons, not worldly weapons, to knock down the strongholds of human reasoning and to destroy false arguments" (2 Corinthians 10:4). Isaiah 26:3 admonishes us to fix our thoughts, thus eliminating *all* guesswork! "Think about things that are excellent and worthy of praise" (Philippians 4:8).

A synonym for *fix* is *cement*. The word *cement* paints a lucid picture of the type of thinking required to win this battle. Loose thoughts are unstable, roaming, unhealthy, and unsettled. In a spiritual battle of light vs. darkness, we cannot permit thoughts to meander anywhere they like.

This reminds me of a story shared by a family member who served in the war. After several days in the field, his company returned to camp for rest and recuperation. While relaxing, one of the soldiers was wounded by a sniper. The camp was well guarded; none had been negligent, yet the enemy had somehow found an opening. Be alert for any word openings. Thank God that His people are well equipped for fighting any battle! Being well equipped for fighting means having the necessary weapons for warfare and having the knowledge to use the weapons. Having weapons and using them strategically are two different things. This can be demonstrated by the indiscriminate use of weapons in the world today.

God has given us a few choice weapons of war, but these are spiritual weapons, not worldly ones. Among these weapons is the powerful Word of God. We use the Word as a weapon by meditating and speaking it aloud. Joshua 1:8 admonishes us to study the Bible, keeping it ever before us. I know this to be so true. We must personally devote time to the Word daily; not giving enough time to the things of God is a surefire way to get lost. The world is replete with snares and traps, and it is a dangerous thing to think we are not vulnerable. Beware of naivety and self-confidence. "So we must listen very carefully to the truth we have heard, or we may drift away from it" (Hebrews 2:1).

The Word is a light that guides us, showing us the way to go, ordering our steps. The Word of God gives us direction. "Your word is a lamp to guide my feet and a light for my path" (Psalm 119:105). However, what good is a weapon if you don't know that you have it or how to use it? Another powerful weapon is the name of Jesus: "You can ask for anything in my name, and I will do it, so that the Son can bring glory to the Father" (John 14:13).

There may be a preponderance of weapons in the world today—assault rifles, missiles, rocket torpedoes, and many other natural weapons—yet they are no match for a believer's God-given weapons. It could, however, be argued that Christians' misuse of words can be compared to the world's misuse of weapons. We fire words like we fire weapons—we load, aim, and shoot! Some hit the intended target while others hit an unintended one doing irreparable damage. *The Word Diet*, in contrast, aims to make you a sharpshooter! As you become more aware of the importance of your thoughts and words, over time, your inner hearing will become acutely sensitive. You will be on high alert for thoughts and words that doubt, criticize, lie, or deny the truth of what the Word of God says about you. You will find yourself saying things such as, "I cast down imaginations!" "I call those words back!" "I rebuke those thoughts!" "I cancel those words!"

The Holy Spirit prompts me every time I find my thoughts roaming in an unfavorable direction. I have learned to question the thought by asking, "Is it true, honorable, right, pure, lovely, or admirable?" If it doesn't meet these biblical prerequisites, I knock it down by speaking to it. The objective is to stop the thought in its tracks; a better way to say it might be to cut the thought off before it leaves any tracks! As you practice this process, it becomes more natural. Soon, you will do it without thinking. Contrary thoughts never cease, but they do become less frequent when you talk back and work against them.

Implementing the following formula can help you shed the heaviness derived from the weight of words. I am certain we all can benefit from putting this aphorism into practice.

Thought Change = **Word** Change = **Behavior** Change = **Life** Change

CHAPTER 4

What Are You Talking About?

We've all heard, "Talk is cheap," but as you have learned thus far, that is certainly not the case! In actuality, talk is expensive and can prove to be very costly. Words carry either faith or fear. Fear is burdensome, but God has promised us rest from the weight of the world; we do not have to bear it alone. If you find yourself using negative verbal exchanges you learned when you were a slave to the world, you are bearing an unnecessary burden of word weight. You are likely speaking words that are wrapped in fear and brought on by the cares of the world and continually rehearsed through unbridled talk.

That old way of talking is weighing you down. Matthew 11:28–30 offers an open invitation to those who desire to be relieved of this heaviness.

> "Come to me, all of you who are weary and carry heavy burdens, and I will give you rest," Jesus promises. "Take my yoke upon you. Let me teach you, because I am humble and gentle at heart, and you will find rest for your souls. For my yoke is easy to bear, and the burden I give you is light."

Though His commandments are not outrageous, they do require submission to God.

People of God, we have a new identity. It could be compared to the witness protection program administered by the U.S. government but with far more protective benefits. The witness protection program establishes a new identity for witnesses to protect those who may be under threat before, during, and after a trial. This new identity includes a new home in a new and different location.

We, too, are witnesses … for God! Our words and our lives are our witness: "Your lives are a letter written in our hearts; everyone can read it and recognize our good work among you" (2 Corinthians 3:2). God provides for us a witness protection program that protects us before, during, and after the trials of life. It too includes a new home, a permanent dwelling promised in John 14:2 in a new location. A far superior advantage exists between the two programs, however; God's program assures us that the perpetrator has been caught and defeated: "He disarmed the spiritual rulers and authorities. He shamed them publicly by his victory over them on the cross" (Colossians 2:14–15).

As a result, we have been acquitted and declared not guilty. We have been set free, and God keeps no record of our misdeed! He does not remember it; it's as though it never existed. In addition to getting a new home and new freedom, God's witness protection program adds a new language, God's language, the language of faith. So why are we acting and speaking as if we were still in captivity?

Do you not know? Have you not heard? We have been transformed, overhauled. We have undergone a heart transplant. During a natural heart transplant, the doctor removes a diseased heart and replaces it with a new donor heart. Amazingly, the new heart comes from a human donor who has died. Similarly, God has done the same thing with us and for us: "And I will give you a new heart, and I will put a new spirit in you. I will take out your stony, stubborn heart and give you a tender, responsive heart" (Ezekiel 36:26). Though our donor (Jesus) died, He rose again! Yes, you can go ahead and shout now!

The survival rates for those who have undergone organ transplants are reportedly growing, but God's transplants are even better—because we get an eternity! "For the wages of sin is death, but the free gift of God is eternal life through Christ Jesus our Lord" (Romans 6:23). "O clap your hands all ye people; shout unto God with the voice of triumph" (Psalm 47:1 NKJV).

For far too long, Christians have been portrayed as a begging and whining people. Day after day, we go to God with the same tune played to a sniveling and pleading melody. We know Jesus is seated at God's right hand, and you can believe He is not tapping His foot to that singsong tune. "He has given me a new song to sing, a hymn of praise to our God" (Psalm 40:3). It is time for us to stand and declare!

We are a new people created in Christ Jesus. We are made just like God, in His image and likeness (Genesis 1:26). Ephesians 1:13 says God "identified you as His own, by giving you the Holy Spirit." Consequently, we need to follow His example. Think about it: every living creature emulates its father. You don't see a dog whinnying like a horse or a horse oinking like a pig. You will, however, find a dog barking like the species that it is, imitating the actions of its father. Dogs bark, cows moo, chickens cluck, God speaks, and we speak. We have the right to talk as God talks because Jesus earned that right for us. Open your mouth! We, the church, have been given authority by the One who has all authority, Jesus!

Speak God's Word and start commanding! Words can be likened to planting a tree, and our words are seeds. Our speaking plants the word seed deep into the soil of our heart. Regular confession waters the word seed that in turn provides life. To produce life, we must speak life, not death. Good seed produces a good harvest, and bad seed produces a bad harvest.

Remember that the tongue has power! God's Word is life: "For the word of God is alive and powerful. It is sharper than the sharpest two-edged sword, cutting between soul and spirit, between joint and marrow. It exposes our innermost thoughts and desires" (Hebrews 4:12).

We must be rooted in love; when that occurs, our talk will be godly. In so many instances, we permit a single word, a few words, or innumerable words to have life-transforming power. This can lead to emotional and physical action. We recently had some landscaping done in our backyard. The landscaper advised us that the roots of a very large tree would choke and prevent the growth of the grass that we desired. Sure enough, the roots had spread throughout the yard, choking the life out of everything in its path. Check your roots!

You may have been cajoled by the words, "I love you." A single word like *cancer* spoken by your doctor can immediately alter your life plans. The word "Fire!" in a theater causes a flurry of frantic activity. "You're fired!" proclaimed by your boss makes your heart pound and your head spin. These are but a few examples of the power of words. If we permit God's Word to do so, it will have overwhelming power. Our victory is only assured when we keep the Word first in our heart and mouths. It is a compelling combatant against the cares of the world.

The Word of God gives us a picture of how God loves us and sees us. We catch hold of this through studying His Word. I would speculate that we don't trust Him because we don't really know Him, so we should get to know Him. Even Christians haltingly apply their faith for lack of knowing the Father. Only through knowing the heavenly Father can we learn to trust Him. We can ascertain from our natural lives that before we can really know or trust someone, we need to develop a relationship with him or her, and that involves time spent with the person. Relationships develop trust. God sees us through eyes of love, compassion, and goodness. When we trust Him, we will begin to see ourselves as He sees us, and this too will transform our speech.

Words whether favorable or unfavorable go deep into the soul, and when we speak, our words leave a mark. Do not participate in conversations that open your mind and heart to the expectations the world says are inevitable. "I will watch what I do and not sin in what I say. I will hold my tongue when the ungodly are around me" (Psalm 39:1). Live by God's Word. Learn to check everything by what God says, and expect God's best. Expectations contribute to results. Remember, talk is not cheap. The fact is that it may cost you dearly!

CHAPTER 5

How Do I Nourish My Spirit?

Eating a proper healthy and well-balanced diet is an essential element for nourishing the material body. However, a truth that may be lesser known is that a well-balanced spiritual diet is equally essential for the nourishment of your spirit. This kind of diet requires feasting daily on the Word of God. Natural diets decrease your intake of calories, while spiritual diets increase your intake of the Word of God.

Did you know that the Bible makes several hundred references to eating? I think we can say with confidence that eating is important to God. Failure to consume healthy, natural nutrition affects how we feel, look, act, and even think. It sets us up for poor health conditions, disease, and possibly a decreased life span. If that is the natural outcome for eating poorly, can you imagine the spiritual consequence of neglecting spiritual food?

The physical digestion process closely parallels the spiritual digestion process. Natural digestion starts as soon as we take the first bite of food. Chewing breaks the food down into bite-sized pieces. Saliva mixes with the food, helping with the breaking-down process so our body can easily absorb and use the nutrients. Finally, the food is swallowed and then digested. The digestive system converts the consumed food into nutrients that the body uses for energy, growth, and cell repair.

Just as the mouth is the beginning of the digestive tract in the physical realm, the mouth is the beginning of digestion in the spiritual realm. God's Word speaks of "eating" the Word, receiving it in our innermost parts. We receive it, store it in our hearts, speak it, and then act on it.

This too is part of the eating process. Spiritual food—the Word of God—provides spiritual nourishment and nutrition for our spiritual growth and development. The Word of God is the "words" of God.

We are composed of spirit, soul, and body as evidenced by the following scripture: "Now may the God of peace make you holy in every way, and may your whole spirit and soul and body be kept blameless until our Lord Jesus Christ comes again" (1 Thessalonians 5:23). It is with our spirit that we worship and communicate with God. "For God is Spirit, so those who worship him must worship in spirit and in truth" (John 4:24). Unfortunately, many people spend their lives feeding the physical but starving the spiritual: "I live because of the living Father who sent me; in the same way, anyone who feeds on me will live because of me. I am the true bread that came down from heaven. Anyone who eats this bread will not die as your ancestors did (even though they ate the manna) but will live forever" (John 6:57–58).

In the natural world, a cleansing of the palate serves to remove the residue of previously eaten foods. A person of epicurean tastes prepares the palate by cleansing after each course, as this enhances the appreciation of taste and flavor for the next bite. Likewise, there can also be a spiritual preparation of the palate. We can indulge in a spiritual preparation of the palate by finding a quiet place to ourselves and shutting the door. You may desire to play music ever so softly—that is, worship music. The music eliminates outside competition and cleanses the atmosphere, removing environmental residue while calming the mind in preparation for the entrance of the Holy Spirit.

Music can help us enter into the presence of God. We are admonished to sing psalms, hymns, and spiritual songs making melody to the Lord in our hearts, giving thanks to God the Father at all times and for everything in the name of Jesus (see Ephesians 5:19). We are invited to come before Him with singing and enter His courts with praise. God may even give you a personal praise song in your heart that you just might find yourself expressing aloud to Him. Praise is powerful!

The Word tells us that God inhabits—He dwells or abides in—the praises of His people (see Psalm 22:3). Praise glorifies the Lord. We could even say that praise feeds Him. God is riding on the breath of our praises! Imagine that! I find that praise leads right into worship. I believe in and experience a difference between praise and worship though many use the terms interchangeably. My definition of worship is best expressed in Psalm 46:10: "Be still, and know that I am God!" God is in the stillness!

Confession of scriptures is another great way to prepare your spiritual palate. A favorite of mine is Psalm 150. Speaking it over and over charges not just the atmosphere but also you. Confessions will aid the digestion of God's Word. You may have heard about food that sticks to your ribs. Well, scriptural confessions are food that sticks to your spirit. When we confess God's Word aloud, spiritual nourishment is received in our deepest parts by "chewing" on that Word. Chewing in the spiritual sense involves voicing the scripture, studying its meaning, turning it over in our minds, praying, thinking, and rethinking on it.

When we dissect the Word in contemplation until the sweet flavor and juices flow out of it, the result is that faith emanates! Confession of God's Word intensifies our praise and worship because our hearts become full of gratefulness, reverential awe, and the wonder of God's majesty! Music and confession allow us to experience a double dose of His majesty like a sweet dessert. I encourage you to play worship music softly while making your confessions. Be forewarned: you may not be able to stand! You may unconsciously drop to your knees and then, just like that, time vanishes. Your hands will automatically rise in submission. Lift up holy hands in prayer and praise the Lord. Lift up your hands and surrender—really surrender! We have no real power to do anything without Him, so we may as well acquiesce. If you think otherwise, convince me. Show me the lab where you keep the breath of life.

Confession is a way to give back to God what He has said. Put Him in remembrance! Speak His Word aloud and make it personal. Put your name in it! Doing so will change the atmosphere and change you! Confessing His Word builds faith on the inside that is voice-activated. When you hear your voice speaking the Word of God, using the breath He provides you, what you speak becomes entirely convincing.

God's Word is food; it is nourishment for our physical and spiritual parts. God's Word is compared to water, honey, milk, bread, and meat. It is sustenance. It provides strength, vitality, growth, and life. Believers can depend on God because He cannot lie. Take Him at His Word because He is the Word! The training manual for believers is the Word of God.

Scripture tells us that a mature believer is able through training to recognize the difference between right and wrong. What does this mean in terms of what we speak? Simply put, a mature believer knows the importance of the tongue. After reading this chapter, you can undoubtedly say with assurance that a diet of God's Word is indeed a diet with more than enough nourishment.

CHAPTER 6

What Happens When I Declare the Word?

The Word of God lets us know that when it is declared, faith is strengthened, God is exalted, and you are communicating your faith.

Your Faith Is Strengthened

So many believers question the will of God for their lives. How do we know God's will? It's in His Word. We know His will when we know His Word because His Word is His will. Declare it. Confess it. He has said it, so we too can boldly say it. Faith is strengthened by the repeated declaration of His Word, so keep saying it.

When I was young, I was diagnosed with type-1 diabetes. I was a believer yet had no understanding of the Truth (God's Word) or how to apply it. Diabetes had a strong history of assault on family members creating a propensity for it. I agreed with the diagnosis; I planted it in my heart and watered it with my words. I was tormented by a fear of diabetic complications, gave meticulous attention to my diet, was a slave to the clock of consistent meal times, never walked barefoot, and wore the embarrassing bulge of a diabetic pump under my clothes. That went on for years. I accepted it as my fate. But then … God! I heard the Truth of Isaiah 53:4–5, 1 Peter 2:24, Exodus 15:26, and Psalm 107:20 and discovered there is a cornucopia of healing in the Word of God.

As I began confessing the Word on healing, the traps of diabetes began falling off. I was miraculously taken off the pump by my doctor. I'm told

I have the blood pressure of a teenager. My eyesight is clear. My feet are healthy. I am as strong as ever. My doctor says I am a wonder. This is an unusual testimony for someone with a long-running diabetes diagnosis. I believe and confess the report of the Lord that I am healed regardless of what any person or test says. Now you see what I mean when I say faith is strengthened by confession of God's Word. You can build faith to dispel fear, defeat sickness, overcome lack, find employment, chase away worry, find peace, and even control weight!

Never stop declaring His Word. Make it drown out every contrary thought, word, or deed. Confession confirms that you believe what God's Son has done for us. Confession will help you manage and take control of your life. Declaring the Word daily builds confidence. It keeps me moving forward. Hearing yourself declaring the Word is a good faith-strengthening practice. Yes, it is important to read the Word, but you must know that the supernatural happens when you get the Word into your spirit and declare it, so say something! Say what is consistent with what God has declared to be true about you. That is how you strengthen your faith.

The Word will become so real in you that you will see it with your mind's eye; it becomes a knowing you can't contain; it has to burst out!

"But if I say I'll never mention the Lord or speak in his name, his word burns in my heart like a fire. It's like a fire in my bones! I am worn out trying to hold it in! I can't do it!" (Jeremiah 20:9)

The world says that seeing is believing, but believers say believing is seeing. You must truly believe unwaveringly. Many ask God for things they want; they know He can deliver, but they don't believe He will, so they don't receive it. The Word of God says we often ask amiss: "And even when you ask, you don't get it because your motives are all wrong—you want only what will give you pleasure" (James 4:3).

God Is Exalted

Declaring God's Word is a praise to Him. It honors His son, Jesus, the Word. Really meditate on what that means. Declaring the Word is to declare Jesus. Additionally, it confirms our belief in all He has done for us. The words coming out of our mouth lift Him up. It pleases Him. Just as a natural father is pleased when good is spoken about his children, the same applies to God, our heavenly Father.

God's Word cancels out the contrary when we decree or command it. Jesus told his disciples, "I have been given all authority in heaven and on earth" (Matthew 28:18). Jesus delegated that same authority to us, the church. We are the church, the body of Christ. Authority figures such as parents, teachers, and police officers make decrees, and their decrees are honored. We are His ambassadors on earth. We can decree with authority and with the full assurance that all heaven is backing us up, guaranteed!

Communicating Your Faith

Making biblical declarations puts you in a place of power. You avail yourself to God, ultimately agreeing with what He has said and done! You are adding your own yes and amen! You are affirming that you do believe though you have yet to see the realization. You are also communicating your faith.

When you make a practice of confessing God's Word, a change takes place in you. In time, you become resolute and convinced that His Word is true. Nothing can dissuade you from the truth of the Word of God, nor can you be persuaded that His Word is not yours, a part of your inheritance. You are the rightful heir. Ironically, though we have subdued animals, beasts, birds, and reptiles, we have yet to tame one of the smallest members of our bodies: our tongues. The Word of God compares the tongue to a rudder that guides a ship. The tongue guides our lives. The utterances from our lips can take us where we want to go or keep us standing still. This is no small matter!

Agreeing with God's Word will help you become unshakable, which is certainly a goal worthy of pursuing. However, it happens only when you know that the Father is with you. I'm told that a well-known gospel teacher and his wife were dining quietly in their home when they received what would be to most devastating news about one of their children. They were unmoved, remaining composed, quietly finishing their meal before they went to attend to their child. This may sound uncaring to some, but to me, it shows unshakable faith. They knew their faith was at work. The gospel teacher and his wife allowed their faith to go to work for them.

They trusted God completely. This incident is reminiscent of how Jesus handled Lazarus's death. He waited several days to go to him knowing what He would do. Faith can be compared to a body muscle. Faith works for us as does a muscle. Muscles help to move our bodies. Faith helps to move whatever we apply it to. Flex your muscle! Let your faith do the work for you.

Take Him at His Word; confess with your mouth and believe in your heart. Isn't that how you were brought to salvation? That is a great miracle. Connect the dots. Believing and confessing brings about miracles, and you are one! When there seems to be no outward evidence of what God said, you are assured that His Word is true, confessing His Word makes it easier to wait for the physical manifestation of His promise. And so we wait in faith with the confidence that what we hope for will happen. It gives us assurance about the things we cannot see.

But know this: our act of declaring His Word does not persuade God to move regardless of the number of times we confess. Confession moves us, not God. Jesus completed what He was sent here to do. He said, "It is finished" (John 19:30). We must say, "If it's to be, it's up to me." We have a role to play.

1. Find out what the Word of God says about your circumstance.
2. Take the Word like a dose of medicine: study and meditate on it.
3. Declare the Word in faith, changing you from the inside, appearing on the outside.

Make confession a conscious practice. There is a learning theory that supports repetition: remember the multiplication tables? How did you learn them? I recall sitting in front of my mother rapidly firing them off from memory after repeating them over and over. As student and educator, I often practiced the use of repetition in the classroom when teaching a new skill. When you rehearse something often enough, you believe it. It becomes a part of you. Practice confession of the Word, repeating it over and over. There truly is power in confession.

CHAPTER 7

How Can I Live Healthy in a Word-Weighted World?

This is a W-O-R-D world. One of the most important things that we do every day is talk. My investigation shows that there are all sorts of talk: talk around … talk away … talk up … talk down … talk in … talk out … talk over … talk radio … talk show … talk therapy … baby talk … back-talk … big talk … small talk … by-talk … chalk talk … cross talk … double talk … fast talk … fight talk … happy talk … pep talk … pillow talk … sales talk … smack talk … smoke talk … sweet talk … table talk … town talk … trash talk … self-talk … sloppy talk …[6] Take a deep breath; that's a lot of talking!

That reason alone made it worthwhile to write a book that talks about talking, and this is that book! *The Word Diet* is a diet of faith talk. The preponderance of talk does not diminish the power of words. Talk is plentiful and yet equally powerful. It truly is everywhere.

Doesn't it seem that there are temptations all around us when we are on a diet whether natural or spiritual? You know how it is! When you are trying to lose weight, someone has a celebration and brings calorie-laden sweets to the office. A friend offers to treat you to a meal at a restaurant that happens to specialize in your favorite fattening food. The delightful smell of buttered popcorn, the vision of cookies in a bakery window, or the smell of bacon wafting into the room where you are dining on a not-so-tasty

---

[6] "talk," Dictionary.com, http://www.dictionary.com/browse/talk.

rye crisp; these all beckon us to partake in the pound-packing, unhealthy goods. The same is true of words.

Unrestrained conversations at the office, the hair salon, and family gatherings are among the many places where we are enticed to indulge in verbal indiscretions. Just like a regular diet, it will take a great deal of discipline to stick to *The Word Diet*. But how does a believer live healthily in a world full of unhealthy words? How do we not succumb to unhealthy words when we are out and about?

We can borrow a few tips from successful dieters who drop excess pounds. They carry nonfattening, healthy snacks along with them to prevent indiscriminate eating. In a like manner, word dieters can carry spiritual snacks suitable to their palate in the form of reading, listening, and viewing materials including but not limited to:

1. Recording daily confessions on all mobile devices (Since you likely carry a mobile phone or tablet, you can always have readily available listening and study materials at your disposal.)
2. downloading a Bible application
3. keeping your study notes from church, Bible classes, and workshops on your mobile devices
4. listening to teaching tapes in your car
5. downloading Word books onto your mobile devices
6. tuning in to video-sharing devices to watch a favorite Word program

I have over twenty audiobooks on my mobile devices, and I listen to them whenever I have downtime. I encourage you to do the same. Take them on vacations and everywhere you go. Since investing in a pair of wireless headphones, I am never without the Word in some form. Technology has expanded the possibilities of being ever ready with the Word. Listening to and concentrating on your recordings blocks worldly noise while sharpening your spiritual senses. Since many of us carry these devices, let's make them work for us! We cannot afford to waste time; Jesus is coming back!

Receive What God Has for You

God's promises must be applied, so don't deny them. The scriptures overflow with them, so receive them! Though most go unclaimed, these promises are our inheritance.

- When God says you are healed—receive it.
- When He says all will work out for you—receive it.
- When He says He will provide for you—accept it.
- When He says He will protect you—abide in Him.
- When He says He loves you—accept his love.
- When He says He will fight for you—let vengeance be His.
- When He says not to worry—don't.
- When He says He is your ability—walk in it.

This is called taking God at His Word. He cannot lie, so whatever He declares, you must declare. God's Word is the instruction manual for life. Sadly, we are not inclined to read instructions. We jump ahead of the instructions thinking, "I've got this!" Only when things fail to work or break down do we seek instruction, and even then, we have the nerve to complain or demand a full refund so to speak. We assume no responsibility for our failure.

Does any of this sound familiar? Is that how we treat the Word of God? Do we consult the Word or the world for guidance? It is incredulous the number of worldly talking personalities giving worldly advice based on worldly opinions. They continue to speak the world's language—everything the world wants to hear—and the world devours it. Conversely, those belonging to God are attentive to His voice. So many Christians confess that they cannot hear God's voice. Are you reading God's Word? Then you do hear His voice!

Be a Word Watcher

Unwanted weight can sneak up on us since most of us eat heedless of calories, carbs, or consequences. Whenever we begin to notice physical weight gain or realize our too-tight fitting clothes are speaking to us, the first thing we should do is examine our diet. Naturally, weight gain occurs when we regularly consume more calories than we burn. We can say the same about word weight. Regularly engaging in excessive, unhealthy language can result in heaviness and lethargy.

We must make it a priority to become word watchers who pay attention to the words we speak. We tend to speak unmindful of the power our words carry and are perplexed when unfavorable circumstances creep into our lives. It would behoove us all to check our daily intake. What are we feasting on? What exactly are we consuming?

Take an honest look and ask yourself, are these things feeding my thoughts and consequently my words? Have I chosen to dine from the *menu à la TV*? Is someone else's vision telling my thoughts what to think or my words what to say? Do I crave certain popular but immoral shows? Does my mouth water as I anxiously anticipate the next episode (i.e., entrée)? Do I TiVo a juicy series to assure I don't miss a single serving? Do I binge on late-night news, talk shows, or celebrity tell-all shows before retiring?

Consider your *menu à la lunchtime*. Ask yourself, am I retaining water-cooler word weight while at work by indulging in toxic conversations? Am I chomping on sandwiches in the lunchroom that contain offensive onion opinions, pungent Limburger lies, or mouthy and meddlesome meat? Am I nibbling on a grumbling granola bar at my desk? Do I use my mobile devices to snack between meals, devouring the day's latest crime-filled news reports, financial woes, or disasters? Is my thirst quenched with hater-ade throughout the day?

We cannot expect to lose word weight when dining from these all-you-can-eat, buffet-style menus any more than we could expect to shed physical pounds while munching on greasy chips, icing-laden cookies, and pound cakes and drinking sugary sodas. We are given a myriad of suggestions to keep our natural weight under control; now let's look at what God says about keeping our word weight under control.

We want to be certain that the light we think we have is not actually darkness. Luke 11:34–36 says to guard our eyes; that means to watch what we watch. "Your eye is a lamp that provides light for your body. When your eye is good, your whole body is filled with light. But when it is bad, your body is filled with darkness" (Matthew 6:22–23). When we are filled with light, our life becomes a floodlight that should be out front where it can be seen, illuminating the world around us, while the glory is given to God.

James 1:19 tells us, "Be quick to listen, slow to speak, and slow to get angry" while Proverbs 20:12 reminds us, "Ears to hear and eyes to see—both are gifts from the Lord." Since God gave us eyes and ears, God knows what we should do with them. He knows what we see and hear will influence us.

Opposites may attract in the world, but the Word says, "Not so fast. The righteous and unbelievers are direct opposites. How can they partner?" (2 Corinthians 6:14). Christians are repeatedly told throughout the scriptures to not team up with unbelievers. Light and darkness cannot coexist. When we feed on the world and all it has to offer, we cannot walk with God. Our directions and destinations are different. We are called the set-apart ones.

As children of God, we are headed in an entirely different direction than the world. We are not ordinary people. We are different; set apart from the world; God calls us a peculiar people. These verses refer to relationships human and nonhuman. They speak to alliances. With whom or what is your alliance? We must ask this of ourselves and answer it truthfully. Birds of a feather do flock together. What we allow ourselves to continuously feed on with our eyes, ears, mouths, or thoughts profoundly affects our lives. A commitment to healthy doses of the Word of God is essential to shed word weight, keep the pounds off, and live healthily in a Word world. Knowing what to do is only effective if we actually do it.

Consider Your Food Source

We have many options when deciding on the source of our food purchases; there are grocery stores, supermarkets, convenience stores, produce stores, delicatessens, and specialty food stores. Many of us shop at a combination of these options. *The Word Diet*, however, procures its food from one source only: God's Word. Knowing this, we don't have to look for brand names, sales, or bargains though unfortunately there are many selling false goods. Your meal is derived from the Word; your meal *is* the Word. You need not shop around. It is written in your heart. You confessed it with your mouth.

The Word of God provides life, health, and healing. It is for these things—life, health, and healing— that we eat naturally and spiritually. So how does a Christian live healthily in a Word world, you ask? By living on a diet of the Word of God: *The Word Diet*.

CHAPTER 8

Become a Back-Talker

When I was a child, my mom taught me not to back-talk when she commanded me to do something—"Just do it!" (You thought Nike came up with that, right?) She considered my childish retorts insolent. That kind of behavior was not allowed in our house, and she would smack me if she heard it. Yeah, I know, but that was back in the day. I was a smart aleck, but her backhand taught me to keep my mouth shut, I have since learned an appropriate use for back-talk.

I recently saw a magazine article entitled "Aging Equals Pain." "Not so!" I said to the article. I did not want that in my psyche, and so I talked back to it. I am careful not to permit what others say is a fact to become the truth in my life. I talk back if whatever it is argues against the truth of the Word of God. That's an appropriate place to say something.

Today, we are bombarded with bad news: crime, disease, war, injustice, unemployment, and every other negativity in the news. Believers, however, can win this assault of bad news with the Good News, the gospel. Say what it says. "It will not touch me," declares Psalm 91. You must know the Word and you must speak the Word. Talk back to fight the fear so prevalent in the world.

It is not surprising to me when I read about a talking reptile or a talking donkey in the Bible, nor am I amazed that Jesus talked to a tree. Haven't we all experienced inanimate objects as well as animals talking to us? The dialogue may not have been apparent or audible to us humans, but it can certainly be heard. Often, the voice of things is louder than any human voice. For example, our bank account talks all the time; why do you think we constantly check to see what it's saying? Our feet talk to us when we have been on them all day, and we answer by getting off them. Likewise, our stomach talks to us when we have not eaten, and our response is to feed it. My dog talks to me by sitting at the door when she wants to go out; I answer by taking her out.

A response is a reply. Jesus responded to the fig tree that had no figs, which means the tree spoke first. Biblical scholars speculate that the tree said, "I have figs." However, that is not to imply that the tree uttered an audible sound. Fig trees produce fruit and leaves simultaneously, and so it spoke through the evidence of leaves, as well as the absence of figs. Evidently, Jesus knew this or He would not have expected figs. When He found the fig tree devoid of figs, Jesus—who was hungry—cursed the tree. What do you say when your bank account tells you it has no money?

I want to make three points here.

1. Someone or something is always speaking to you.
2. Start listening.
3. Talk back!

Whenever I am presented with a challenge, I speak to it in the name of Jesus. I talk back to it! I know and believe God's Word. It assures me that faith-filled words will deliver victory. Yes, I talk to things, and you can and should also. Exercise your dominion as a believer. Jesus tells us to speak to mountains. If your situation is talking to you and countering God's Word, talk back to it! Confidently say what God has said about it. Call it as you desire it to be. Your words are creative. Speak! Stand! Command! I am not telling you what I heard; I'm telling you what I know.

I accidentally closed a kitchen drawer on my finger, which was painful. I spoke to the pain in the name of Jesus: "Pain, I am speaking to you: I refuse *all* pain. I am redeemed from pain!" That was it! The pain left immediately. I forgot about the incident until sometime later when I went to get a manicure. My nail technician remarked that I had a bruise under my nail; I had not noticed it due to the lack of pain. It was her remark that brought the bruise to my attention, and only then did I recall the incident. This is key: speak and forget it. Don't try to provoke an outcome by continually checking the results.

On another occasion, I was moving too quickly in the kitchen and inadvertently grabbed a hot pan with my ungloved hand. Immediately the pain came, and immediately I rebuffed the pain by speaking to it. The throbbing left just as quickly as it came without as much as a blister. Naturally, this is not what happens when you grab a hot pan! It's not natural, it's supernatural!

Put the Word to Work

If I am unable to find something, I put the Word to work by asserting it. I don't call anything lost because my faith knows that nothing is lost to the Spirit, who is my Helper. I say, "Holy Spirit, You know where it is; reveal it to me." Invariably, He will do just that. My husband, formerly a skeptic, has witnessed this so often until he now believes it and acts on it too!

One day, my husband could not find his cell phone despite looking everywhere for it while I was asleep. He awakened me to ask if I had seen it. He'd dialed the number but hadn't heard it ring. I said, "Let's ask the Holy Spirit." We did, and then we went to bed. The next morning, he went outside to walk the dog. At that time, he wasn't looking for his phone there; he never suspected it could be outside. Instead, he found the phone outside protected underneath a tree. It is important to note that it had rained hard that night. Thank you, Jesus!

On another occasion, I had a business appointment in a town I had never been to. Though I put the address in my cellphone, I discovered I didn't have my phone when I arrived in town. No cellphone, no address! Panic attempted to converse with me by saying, "You drove all this way and don't have an address!" I verbally countered by saying, "Holy Spirit, show the address to me."

About that time, I noticed a parking space. I pulled into the space intending to look through my purse once again for my phone. To my amazement, when I looked up, I saw that the sign on the door of the building where I had parked was the business I was looking for! I realize this may sound far out to some, and yes, it is far out—far outside the realm of your experience. Some say that experience is the best teacher, but I'm here to tell you that isn't necessarily so. There are many truths outside our experiences.

We tend to speak evil of the things we do not understand. If we haven't personally experienced something, we may rule it out entirely, even ridicule it; consider the great ideas that were initially ridiculed but later proved to be true. Nonetheless, I am telling you what I have experienced: "I assure you, we tell you what we know and have seen, and yet you won't believe our testimony" (John 3:11). Why do we take the evidence of man at face value and stumble at the testimony of God? (See 1 John 5:9). We exalt our experience above God's Word, and that ought not to be. I know who I am; I know what I believe, and that's all I need to know. I admit my results are not always consistent. I also realize that any failure has to do with me, not God, as He is consistency itself. I still subscribe to the Word: "Because of your faith, it will happen" (Mark 9:29).

Begotten Son

I heard the story of the cross many times as a child beginning in Sunday school, and the emphasis was always on sin. I had been taught only that Jesus took our sins likely because we all want to go to heaven. However, it wasn't until much later that I received the revelation of what happened spiritually. Once I understood exactly what took place at the crucifixion of Jesus in the spiritual realm, it changed my life.

He did take on our sins, but there is more to it than that. He took upon Himself sin, shame, sickness, pain, grief, sorrow, lack—represented by nakedness—and death. He took all these conditions so that through faith we would no longer have to carry them. The Holy Spirit suddenly gave this revelation to me so clearly one day that I will never forget it. It was so impactful. It was a word spoken specifically to me and for me by the Holy Spirit. In my spirit, I very precisely heard, "What does it mean when someone takes something from you? It's gone! You no longer have it in your possession. If they return for it, you say: I don't have it." That settled it for me!

Jesus did not die on the cross simply to become the most historically significant person as some have deemed Him. There was a much more significant reason for His sufferings; He did it for us because He loves us:

"For God loved the world so much that he gave his one and only Son, so that everyone who believes in him will not perish but have eternal life" (John 3:16). He did it for love: "There is no greater love than to lay down one's life for one's friends" (John 15:13). What manner of man is this!

Subsequently, we have difficulty accepting so great a love. Because we have not experienced this kind of love, it is assumed by many to be a falsehood. But now that I know these truths, I refuse anything less. My thinking is renewed. As a result, I talk differently. If pain, sickness, shame, lack, grief, sorrow, or even death threatens me, I rise up and reprimand it in Jesus's name!

In the physical world, we would take affront if we were asked to pay for something that had already been purchased. Jesus paid the price—our price—with His blood. Pull out your receipt—the blood—and wave it in the face of the one who is accusing you day and night of having no right to it! Why pay when you don't have to? Better yet, I countermand those words and change them from an interrogative to a declarative statement: "Don't pay when you don't have to!"

When you are being spiritually attacked, that is not the time to keep silent; talk back! Say, "Don't even try it! It's been paid for, and I have the receipt!" Hallelujah! Believers have been given a gift that no one but Jesus could give. He took care of every detail of our lives; He thought of everything and provided everything. It is literally unforgivable not to accept it.

Speak Life

When I wake, even before my feet touch the floor, I begin my talking. I purpose to speak to the day before it speaks to me. The first thing I say is, "Thank you, Lord, for giving me sweet sleep during the night and waking me up this morning. I am grateful." I continue my declarations in preparation for the day's activities. Every expression includes affirmative words that cover family, health, accomplishment, success, energy, wisdom, favor, and whatever else the Holy Spirit gives me to address that day: "I am successful! I am fruitful. I will accomplish everything I need to accomplish today. I have a surplus of energy. I am sound of mind, body, and spirit."

I continue with my faith statements; saying them aloud, I go to the bathroom mirror all the while looking and speaking to myself, "Good morning, Theresa. Today is the best day of your life. You'll get stronger, wiser, healthier, and more attractive every day." And it is so!

Repetition supports learning, but faith alone teaches you to trust. Throughout my day, I find myself talking back to various circumstances with more statements of faith declarations. Sometimes, my responses shock me; I turn around to see who said that! The Word arises spontaneously because it is a part of me.

When you consistently apply the Truth, the Truth will make you free (see John 8:32). The simple fact that men fight and die for what they believe to be freedom proves the value we place on liberty. The sad part about it is that the same strength of desire for spiritual liberty, through the gospel—the Truth— does not exist in most. Knowing Truth will change how you look at people, things, and self. It will do the same with how you feel, the result being a fresh perspective based on the alignment of your words with God's Word. In essence, words paint pictures. Ask yourself, "What picture are my words painting for me?"

Words amid Technology

There are so many voices in the world today, and all are competing for our attention. Words seemingly have a more impactful influence in our lives today than ever before as new and better ways to communicate become available. Words carry such importance that we find it necessary to use devices that enable talking everywhere. These devices are carried not just to facilitate business but also for entertainment.

The use of computers, cell phones, tablets, the Internet, TV, radio, email, online chat rooms, blogs, video calls, and social networking platforms have caused an upsurge in our ability to communicate. Hence, technology makes it easy for mouths to speak and ears to hear. They permit connection possibilities that had not previously been available. One would be hard pressed to go through a day without seeing a cellphone or wireless device in someone's hand. As the popularity of smartphones increases, communication opportunities also increase, which means there are more opportunities to engage in sloppy talk.

We have to learn to make meticulous choices about everything we say to remain faithful and finish this race triumphantly. The Word must become our daily focus. We are responsible for our lives, and our words create our lives. For so long, the culture we live in has been the model for our lives. We've been trained in worldly ways since birth, so it may take some time to peel off the layers the world has loaded onto our backs. It's a constant shedding. Just remember that when the world talks to you, talk back!

CHAPTER 9

Equipping *The Word Diet* Kitchen

The kitchen is one of the busiest rooms in the home, and it is a favorite gathering place for friends and family. Likely, it's because the kitchen is where the food is stirred up. How appropriate is it that we should have a user-friendly, well-equipped, and organized kitchen? This requires certain staples, training, and duties. As family and friends gather in *The Word Diet* kitchen, feel free to share the recipes herein with them.

Organizing Yourself

The knowledge, skills, and abilities needed at the onset of *The Word Diet* are a teachable spirit, a positive mind-set, open-mindedness, and objectivity accompanied by a sincere desire to lose the word weight that stands between you and your God-given destiny.

Duties

- Clean out all unrighteousness.
- Fan into flames your spiritual gifts.
- Destroy strongholds that cause wavering.
- Have willingness to carry the sweet fragrance of the Word of God
- Suit yourself with spiritual armor to deflect the enemy's fiery darts.
- Devote time to prayer, worship, meditation, and studying the Word of God.

Training

Depend on the all-knowing and all-wise Holy Spirit as your teacher and helper. Invite Him into your affairs. Expect Him to give you wisdom without deprecation.

Utensils

- Armor of God: helmet of salvation, breastplate of righteousness, sword of the Spirit, truth for the loins, and peace of the gospel for the feet.
- Weapons of warfare: the name of Jesus, the Word, the blood, the Holy Spirit, praise, prayer, and testimonies.
- Special vessels of honor cleansed and sanctified for God's use.

Staples

Bread

Bread is a staple in our daily lives. God's Word is referred to as bread, and Christ said, "I am the Bread of Life. Whoever comes to me will never be hungry again. Whoever believes in me will never be thirsty" (John 6:35). There is no comparison between the bread we eat and Jesus, the Bread of Life. Jesus feeds the soul while natural bread feeds the body. Jesus does a better and more complete job of nourishing, sustaining, and supporting the body than any variety of natural bread could ever do. No other Bread will satisfy for life! *The Word Diet* encourages you to eat the Bread of Life and never hunger again.

The Bread of Life satisfies our physical thirst and natural hunger; it is the remedy for the overeating we do with words that subsequently weigh us down. In the natural world, bread is eaten at nearly every meal and is even snacked upon. If others—particularly in the dieting arena—were aware of the Bread of Life that satisfies forever, they would surely hunger for it more than they do wheat, brioche, pumpernickel, or sourdough.

Bread is associated with provision or support especially of one's family. "I'm the breadwinner in this house." "I'm responsible for putting bread on the table." Let's take a bite from the Bread of Life here.

> Yes, he humbled you by letting you go hungry and then feeding you with manna, a food previously unknown to you and your ancestors. He did it to teach you that people do not live by bread alone; rather, we live by every word that comes from the mouth of the Lord. (Deuteronomy 8:3)

Jesus said,

> I tell you the truth, Moses didn't give you bread from heaven. My Father did. And now he offers you the true bread from heaven. The true bread of God is the one who comes down from heaven and gives life to the world. (John 6:32–33)

> Anyone who eats the bread from heaven, however, shall never die. I am the living bread that came down from heaven. Anyone who eats this bread will live forever; and this bread, which I will offer so the world may live, is my flesh. (John 6:50–51)

Honey

The Word of God has been described as sweeter than honey. In the natural world, honey provides carbohydrates the body uses for energy and strength. Honey is also credited with improving endurance just as God's people get their strength and endurance from the sweet savor of His Word. Honey is sweet, pleasant tasting, and savory, and so is the Word of God. In a like manner, *The Word Diet* advocates the use of the sweetness of God's Word as a smart choice for your spiritual sweet tooth.

Here in *The Word Diet* kitchen, our goal is to lose weight: word weight. Rather than binge on the alluring, sucrose-laden confections of the world, purpose in your heart to replace negative verbal indulgences with the sweetness of God's Word. Snack on some savory bites of honey from the Word of God: "How sweet your words taste to me; they are sweeter than honey" (Psalm 119:103). "Reverence for the LORD is pure, lasting forever. The laws of the LORD are true; each one is fair. They are more desirable than gold, even the finest gold. They are sweeter than honey, even honey dripping from the comb" (Psalm 19:10).

Milk

God's Word is milk. There was a time when parents were advised that every child needed milk. At that time, most children drank cow's milk. Over the years, it seems that views have changed about milk, and there are a variety of milks to choose from today. There is a great deal of confusing information about the type of milk that is best for human consumption. Allow me to eliminate the confusion with a recommendation of the milk of God's Word.

The Bible references milk for feeding "babies" (those unskilled in the Word). In this instance, the term *baby* alludes to spiritual rather than physical maturity. A milk drinker is one who is inexperienced or unlearned. You may have started out as a milk drinker in *The Word Diet* not yet realizing the importance of the words you speak. By now, you have likely become an eater of solid food. Even so, let's sip some of the appetizers from the milk menu of God's Word.

> For someone who lives on milk is still an infant and doesn't know how to do what is right. (Hebrews 5:13)

> Like newborn babies, you must crave pure spiritual milk so that you will grow into a full experience of salvation. Cry out for this nourishment, now that you have had a taste of the Lord's kindness. (1 Peter 2:2–3)

> I had to feed you with milk, not with solid food, because you weren't ready for anything stronger. And you still aren't ready. (1 Corinthians 3:2)

Meat

The meat of God's Word is for a more seasoned believer who may have been "eating" the Word for a while. Today, in the natural world, many are reluctant to eat meat. "For instance, one person believes it's all right to eat anything. But another believer with a sensitive conscience will eat only vegetables" (Romans 14:2). However, you need not hesitate to eat the meat prepared from God's throne room table.

The spiritual meat from the Word is a healthy addition to the diet of a mature Christian. God's Word can be considered as a meat that is good for you. Solid food, "meat," pertains to spiritual maturity just as "milk" implies being a babe in Christ. Infants are not born with the ability to eat or digest solid food right away. The same may be applied to the believer who is new in the Word. Consuming meat requires having teeth to bite and chew. Feeding meat to an infant too soon may cause the child to choke. And if perhaps the meat made its way down to their unadulterated tummies, their stomachs would reject it one way or another. Infants simply cannot tolerate a solid meal. Some people cannot tolerate God's Word either, but not for the same reason an infant cannot tolerate strong meat.

Some people may refuse to taste the Word for no real reason at all. That person likely has what the Bible refers to as a hardened heart: a heart that is likened to a stone, petrified. Another reason frequently offered is, "I can't understand the Bible." Even more feel it is outdated and not for today's world. Whatever the reason, God desires that no one perishes or be separated from Him eternally. Regardless, humanity has been given the freedom to choose.

The mature Christian will come to enjoy strong meat. In *The Word Diet* kitchen, we bid you to come dine on the Word of God. We invite you to sink your teeth into God's Word.

Water

Water is essential for life. The human body is composed primarily of water. Experts report that a human can live a mere three days without water. Jesus, the Living Water, is the giver of eternal life.

The Word Diet kitchen is fully organized and stocked with nonperishable ingredients that will create scrumptious recipes for your soul. Now that you have completed your basic training, you are ready to work with kitchen power tools! Part 2 contains the power tools that will help you prepare *The Word Diet* ingredients. Let's check them out!

PART II

The Word Diet Power Tools

CHAPTER 10

The Word Diet Exchange System

Power Tool 1: *The Word Diet* Exchange System

In the natural world, a food diet exchange system is a table of foodstuffs with listings of caloric and carbohydrate content that can be used by anyone but is notably useful for those with particular health or weight issues. It provides healthy food choices that can be substituted for less-suitable, fattening, and unhealthy foods.

Much like the description above, *The Word Diet* exchange system is similar in that it provides a choice of favorable words that can be exchanged for the negative and self-containing words spoken against ourselves. The chart below is merely an example and is not by any means conclusive.

Word Exchange Module

UNFAVORABLE WORDS	EXCHANGE FOR...	BASED ON
I'm broke...I don't have any money.	My God supplies all of my needs.	PHIL. 4:19
I'm good for nothing.	I can do all things through Christ.	PHIL. 4:13
I'm worried, afraid or nervous.	I'm anxious about nothing.	PHIL.: 4:6
I can't remember; I'm old and tired.	My judgement and strength are exceptional.	DEUT. 34:7
I can't keep the weight off.	I discipline my body.	1 COR. 9:27
I had an awful day.	I forget the past and look to what lies ahead.	PHIL. 3:13
I can't stand him / her / my boss.	I have the love of God in my heart.	ROM. 5:5
I'm too lazy to exercise.	I will see the rewards of my discipline.	HEB. 12:11

CHAPTER 11

The Word Diary

Power Tool 2: The Word Diary

The Word diary teaches you to keep a written record of unfavorable words. Writing down what you say is a means of tracking hurtful words and identifying negative speaking patterns. Use the template provided to create your own Word diary as this will help you take a critical look at your speaking habits in an effort to assist you with making productive changes.

The Word diary is designed to give you a general picture of who, what, when, where, and why you speak as you do. The more information you gather, the better your chance at losing the weight of unfavorable, unhealthy, and unfruitful words. To start, the goal is to track your words for at least three to five days. An optional but helpful practice is to note the environments that encourage an ungoverned tongue.

How to Make and Maintain Your Word Diary

There are two methods provided for keeping record of your verbal communication pattern; choose what works best for you. You may opt to write down your actual words or use a tally mark system as described in the modules below.

Method 1: Write Your Words

1. *Listen* to yourself as you speak throughout the day.
2. *Jot down* every unfavorable remark under the Unfavorable column.

3. *Examine* your Word diary at the end of each day noting unfavorable words.

4. *Find* what scripture says about that situation.

5. *Rewrite* the unfavorable remarks (according to scripture) in the Revision Column.

6. *Fill* the Based On column with the appropriate scripture, chapter, and verse.

Speak the favorable revisions over yourself. Reading your revisions aloud will create an entirely new recipe or declaration that builds up rather than tears down. Putting the revisions in paragraph form creates new images and gives you a full picture or expanded view of how you should see yourself and your circumstance now.

Eliminate from your vocabulary any unfavorable words you cannot exchange. Practice this exercise until you automatically speak favorably about yourself. How badly do you want to create a new image? That will determine your effort.

Method 2: Tally Mark System

1. *Listen* to yourself as you speak throughout the day.

2. *Make* a tally mark under the unfavorable column for every unfavorable remark made.

3. *Count* the tally marks at the end of each day.

4. *Compare* the number of tally marks each day in the hopes of diminishing them over time.

5. *Reduce* the number of tally marks daily thus reducing the number of unfavorable remarks spoken.

The Word Diary

DAY	UNFAVORABLE WORDS	FAVORABLE REVISIONS	BASED ON

CHAPTER 12

The Word Diet: "Free Foods"

Power Tool 3: The Word Diet "Free Foods"

Typical diets often provide a list of calorie-free foods. Free foods are foods that cost nothing in terms of weight gain. You may indulge in them freely and in unlimited amounts. Often, they add nutrient value but remain calorie free. *The Word Diet* offers a list of free spiritual ingredients that are healthy and non-weighty. Check that you have them available prior to beginning *The Word Diet* and feel free to use them lavishly in every recipe. The following menu items are absolute must-haves!

- Faith: The most imperative ingredient of all!

   o Every concoction in *The Word Diet* kitchen depends on faith to be successful; without it, the result will prove fruitless.
   o It's just like baking bread; if you omit the yeast, the dough won't rise and the bread will be ruined. The same is true of faith: "And it is impossible to please God without faith" (Hebrews 11:6).

- Patience: Several Bible verses speak of patience as a fundamental ingredient in the life of a Christian.

   o In this age of multitasking where we are required to accomplish many things simultaneously, patience has a bad name. "We want it now!" is the prevailing attitude of the world as well as believers.

○ We are already equipped with patience, as it is a fruit of the Spirit received at our new birth. We just need to rekindle it: "But the fruit of the Spirit is love, joy, peace, longsuffering, gentleness, goodness, faith" (Galatians 5:22, NKJV).

○ One of the main ingredients in patience is longsuffering, which may seem bitter to the taste buds and unpleasant to the palate, but it does promote good health.

○ Patience is a force that will push us through. Trust God; patience develops strength of character that leads to confident hope (see Romans 5:4).

• Perseverance: Because we have separated ourselves from the world and have chosen *not* to indulge in worldly ways, we may be taunted, criticized, condemned, and even attacked.

○ There will be pain—not necessarily physical pain but pain nonetheless. Notably, persecution can be as mentally and psychologically painful as physical pain.

○ Be dedicated to the task at hand: "So let's not get tired of doing what is good. At just the right time we will reap a harvest of blessing if we don't give up" (Galatians 6:9).

○ James 1:12 states: "God blesses those who patiently endure testing and temptation. Afterward they will receive the crown of life that God has promised to those who love him."

I know a little about persevering in the natural sense. Just recently, I ran a 10k race. Though I successfully completed a half-marathon previously and had easily completed a practice run on the same course a few days earlier, the experience was quite different this time around. I experienced pain throughout the run; it was a challenge physically and mentally. I was challenged mentally because my mind began telling me I couldn't make it. I had to start talking back by confessing various appropriate scriptures about ultimately persevering in spite of the difficulty. I crossed the finish line! I prevailed and received my medal. I liken that experience to running this spiritual race to the end to obtain a reward, but I do realize that God's reward for us is far greater. The lesson *here* is, don't quit. Persevere!

- Gratitude: Use gratitude with a heavy hand in all of the recipes.

  o Thankfulness (gratitude) is obligatory because it honors and acknowledges God: "And whatever you do or say, do it as a representative of the Lord Jesus, giving thanks through him to God the Father" (Colossians 3:17).
  o The Bible tells a tale of ten lepers who were cleansed by Jesus, but only one turned to say, "Thank you" (see Luke 17:11–19).

I love one verse of a song entitled "I Am the One" by Kurt Carr: "I had to come back, my heart made me run back and tell you thank you." That lyric precisely expresses my sentiments. It is unimaginable to me how some walk around thankless, feigning to not see the hand of God. The whole earth cries of His presence. He is everywhere!

As a runner, I am outdoors nearly every day. I run through a forest preserve, and each year, I observe as the tree leaves turn from bright green to yellow, orange, red, and brown and then fall off. Sometimes, the trees are so thick with foliage that I can barely see the sky. Having taken in the beautiful creations of God, it does not take long for me to see more clearly even through the forest as the trees shed their leaves in preparation for yet another season.

I become more acutely aware of just how short this earthly life really is. I watch the river flowing seemingly on its own, but I know better. I feel the breeze change from a subtle whisper on my neck to a forceful wind. No man can see the wind, only feel it. What manner of man chooses not to believe there is no God behind it all?

I am thankful every day, and I tell this to my Father. I thank Him for the ability to be outdoors, for life, for the ability not just to move but to run and to behold His glory in every nook and cranny of the outdoors. I am grateful!

- Diligence: Diligence is an application of the dogged determination to accomplish your goal with reliance on God.

    ○ Diligence is a cousin to perseverance. We are encouraged to persevere with diligence: "I have fought the good fight, I have finished the race, and I have remained faithful" (2 Timothy 4:7).

    ○ Your part in this diet is the application of diligence.

    ○ Regardless of the circumstances and no matter what something appears to be, diligently say what the Word says. God has already provided.

    ○ Earnestness, intensity, constancy, and attention are synonymous with diligence. You can easily apply this principle to *The Word Diet*; it works if you work it.

• Praise: No recipe is complete without praise; it enhances the flavor of every dish especially if you need a little sweetness.

    ○ We are encouraged to offer a sacrifice of praise: "Therefore, let us offer through Jesus a continual sacrifice of praise to God, proclaiming our allegiance to his name" (Hebrews 13:15).

    ○ We are commanded to praise God: "I tell you that, if these should hold their peace, the stones would immediately cry out" (Luke 19:40 NKJV).

Some cooks say they add a little sweetness to every recipe; they claim it makes everything taste better. I say the same about praise: praise carries sweetness. Praise is another way to show gratitude full of faith and confidence. You don't have to wait until you see the evidence of victory; praise now. Shout the praises of God; shout out the glory of God! Praise Him in the midst of trials. Praise Him for the answer. I have tried to name everything I can think of praising God for, but there is just so much to name that I haven't finished yet!

CHAPTER 13

Anointed Activity Guidelines

Power Tool 4: Anointed Activity Guidelines

Research shows that anointing was an activity engaged in by shepherds tending to their sheep. In this instance, shepherds would pour oil (anoint) on a sheep's head to prevent insects from burrowing into the sheep's ears that could result in its death. This practice became symbolic of blessing, protection, and empowerment.[7] It is of particular interest that the practice of anointing involved shepherds and sheep as Christ is called the Good Shepherd and we are called His sheep. He promises to bless, protect, and empower us just as shepherds in the natural world are expected to care for their sheep.

Physical activity is known to accelerate natural weight loss; it speeds up the body's rate of converting food into energy. Comparably, the anointed activities used in *The Word Diet* module help to speed up the loss of word weight so that we are ready for use by the Lord. Consider

1. the movement of lips in prayer and confession,
2. the bending of knees as we go before God to seek His face, and
3. the lifting of hands in surrender to Him.

All of these activities convey anointing: the protection, the blessing, and empowerment of God the Father. Each greatly expedites the desired

---

[7] Rasbeary.

loss of word weight. Any form of exercise requires discipline, including spiritual exercise. Devote a time of prayer just as you set aside time for exercising at the gym or in your home.

What better way to begin your day than with the anointed activities described in *The Word Diet*? Adding spiritual exercise to your daily regimen could move you closer to an actual physical fitness routine in the natural world. Note the symmetry of physical, bodily activity with that of the spiritual activity of prayer; both have the ability to do the following.

- sustain life
- enhance mood
- assist with sleep
- enhance health
- strengthen

Admittedly it can be challenging to carve out time for any type of regular activity, physical or spiritual. Ask the Lord to help you! Believe me when I say you won't regret it.

PART III

The Word Diet Power Recipes

Recipe Instructions

All recipes contain two parts: ingredients and preparation.

Ingredients

The ingredients consist of scripture from God's Word.

Preparation

1. Read the ingredients and make the declarations aloud. The recommendation is to declare them upon rising in the morning and/or before retiring for the night.
2. Turn (repeat) the declarations over and over with the tongue until faith in the contents is developed and manifestation follows.

Study and meditate on the scriptures associated with the declarations. Reading them in context will be of great assistance to you. After you have done this, stand and let the Word do the work!

CHAPTER 14

Recipe for Employment

Ingredients

1. Psalm 90:17: "And may the Lord our God show us his approval and make our efforts successful. Yes, make our efforts successful!"
2. Ephesians 3:20: "Now all glory to God, who is able, through his mighty power at work within us, to accomplish infinitely more than we might ask or think."
3. Genesis 12:2: "I will make you into a great nation. I will bless you and make you famous, and you will be a blessing to others."
4. Colossians 1:27: "For God wanted them to know that the riches and glory of Christ are for you Gentiles, too. And this is the secret: Christ lives in you. This gives you assurance of sharing his glory."
5. Proverbs 14:23a:"Work brings profit, but mere talk leads to poverty!"
6. Luke 18:1: "I always pray and never give up."

Preparation

Declare: The Word is working mightily in me to produce results.

I see ability in me. I am not disquieted, for God gives me strength to do all things. My faith does not give up! I am fully convinced that my footsteps are ordered by God. I am a competent worker. The Lord rewards the work of my hands with plenty. Therefore, I will to find employment that offers me favorable compensation, (Fill in with your desires.) and infinitely more than I might ask or think. I ask seriously, seek earnestly, and knock confidently believing that my earnest prayer will open the door to my employment.

All things are mine. I refuse to struggle. I function in the glory of God. Jesus in me makes me distinguished among men. Whatever the job requires, I can do it because of the greater One in me. I am successful in everything I do. God gives me grace to excel in everything I do. I am number one. I have the mind of Christ. God has made me a wonder to others. Everything I touch prospers. I am sound.

I contain a seed of greatness. Greatness resides in me. God makes my name great. I am a blessing to others. I cannot fail. I never fail. Failure is not in me because there is no failure in God. I know who I am. I am not an ordinary man because Christ lives in me. I have an, "I can do," mentality. I believe therefore I receive employment now.

CHAPTER 15

Recipe for Health

Ingredients

1. Philippians 4:6: "Don't worry about anything; instead, pray about everything. Tell God what you need, and thank him for all he has done."

2. James 4:7: "So humble yourselves before God. Resist the devil, and he will flee from you."

3. 1 Peter 2:24: "He personally carried [my] sins in his body on the cross so that [I] can be dead to sin and live for what is right. By his wounds [I am] healed."

4. Galatians 3:13: "Christ redeemed us from the curse of the law by becoming a curse for us, for it is written: Cursed is everyone who is hung on a pole."

5. Romans 8:2: "And because you belong to him, the power of the life-giving Spirit has freed [me] from the power of sin that leads to death."

6. John 8:12: "Jesus spoke to the people once more and said, 'I am the light of the world. If you follow me, you won't have to walk in darkness, because you will have the light that leads to life.'"

7. Psalm 89:34: "No, I will not break my covenant; I will not take back a single word I said."

Preparation

Declare: The Word is working mightily in me to produce results.

I am born again by the Word. I have absolute liberty from all forms of oppression from the devil. The devil is not a factor in my body, my life, or my circumstances. He has no power over me. He is defeated. I refuse to fear. I refuse to be anxious or worried. I am the light of the world. Darkness and light cannot exist in the same place, so sickness cannot exist in my body. I refuse every manner of sickness, disease, destruction, and death. I am the custodian of this body; therefore, I command it to comply with the Word of God that I speak to it: "Body, I agree with the Word of God that calls you healed, whole, and well." What Jesus did on the cross cannot be undone. I will never be sick another day in my life. I am sound in mind, body, and spirit. I refuse sickness. I am strong. I believe in the Word of God that says I am healed. If He said it, I believe it. It is finished!

My body glorifies God. Any deadly thing I may have consumed is neutralized by the blood of Jesus. It cannot ravage, tear up, or break down my body's defenses. My body is the temple of the Holy Spirit, so in Jesus's name, I command every cell of my body to comply with the Word of God that says that I am healed, whole, and well. Body, I am speaking to you in the name of Jesus. You are under obligation to respond to the Word of God that I speak.

I am freed from the torments of the destroyer because Jesus is my ransom. I refuse all suffering because Jesus has already suffered in my stead. None of the diseases ravaging the world can follow me ever again. If Jesus doesn't have it, I don't have it. I have supernatural strength. All the weakness and sickness in me dies, and life becomes increasingly more buoyant every day. I take on the strength of Christ.

God has complete healing for me physically, spiritually, and emotionally. I have an amazing, healthy life. All the systems of my body are in perfect order. I am set apart from the sickly world I live in. Any form of poison responsible for blindness, deafness, stomach disorders, chest problems, heart disease, blocked arteries, strokes, cancer, diabetes, Alzheimer's, and every form of bodily poison is swallowed up in victory by the blood of Jesus.

(For those with a cancer diagnosis who have received an evil report, please know and say this.)

The diagnosis may be a fact, but it is not the truth. I believe the report of the Lord that says I am healed. I am not anxious or worried about anything. I am calm and undisturbed. I refuse to fear. I am sound. I have great peace in knowing that nothing is too hard for God. God's eternal life in me has creative, restorative, and preservative power. I use my tongue to command a blessing upon this body: in the name of Jesus, I choose life, and I speak the life of God to every part of my body. Sickness will not lord it over me. According to Isaiah 53:5, I am healed. I will live and not die. I reclaim my health.

Cancer is a curse, and I refuse it. I am redeemed from every curse of the law. I resist cancer. It cannot stay. Cancer cannot ravage, tear up, or break down my body's defenses. Radiation, chemotherapy, or any other treatment cannot ravage, tear up, or break down my body's defenses. I will suffer no form of breakdown in my body. No disease can consume my flesh or make my bones stick out. God has rescued me from the grave (Job 33:21–24).

The scriptures that declare God's desires for His children's wellness are profuse. We have a role to play in our health. One of the biggest rascals in a cancer diagnosis is fear. Do all you can to avoid fear. Fear will shut down the faith necessary for the healing power in the Word. In Deuteronomy 30:15, we are offered the choice of life or death. We can speak life or we can speak death. The above recipes are full of the God-breathed life of God. Take them as your own as you would a medicine prescribed by your physician and be well! See yourself well!

CHAPTER 16

Recipe for Longevity

Ingredients

1. Psalm 91:16: "I will reward them with a long life and give them my salvation."
2. Proverbs 11:28: "The righteous will flourish like the green leaf."
3. Job 5:26: "I will go to the grave at a ripe old age, like a sheaf of grain harvested at the proper time!"
4. Psalm 92:14: "Even in old age they will still produce fruit; they will remain vital and green."
5. Ruth 4:15a: "May he restore your youth and care for you in your old age."

Preparation

Declare: The Word is working mightily in me to produce results.

I am strong and ever flourishing. The Lord restores me day by day making me stronger, healthier, and wiser. He refreshes my being. I will suffer no form of breakdown in my body. My eyes see clearly without artificial aid. My knees are not troublesome but bend easily and readily to give honor and glory to God.

My mind is sound. I retain what I read. I remember all I need to remember. I have something to say about my life, and I agree with the Word of God for a long, healthy, and prosperous life. I will not die until I am satisfied. I am connected to the vine. I will not wither and dry up. I am a tree of righteousness. I am like a tree planted by the rivers of water that bring life, health, and strength. My roots are sunk into the very river of God. I cannot be moved. The Lord my God will always provide a way of escape, turning the bad into good regardless of how it may look. I trust Him. He gives me daily wisdom that is more precious to me than anything. God's Word is stored in my heart. As I speak it in faith, it will surely come to pass.

I am not an ordinary man/woman. I am God's child, a member of His family. God, who is the Vine, is in me, and I, a branch, am in Him (see John 15:5). My life is with Christ. I abide in Him and bear much fruit. I will not wither or dry up. Even in old age, I prosper. I am never alone. I am never lonely. He is with me always. He keeps my feet (see Proverbs 3:26). I will not stumble or fall. I refuse to live in fear or dread. I trust Him, the Giver of Life.

Today more than ever, it seems that we are on a quest to find the elusive fountain of youth. If a fountain of youth exists at all, it is in our mouths; it is our words. Christians are too close to the forest to see the trees. What are we communicating? This cannot be expressed enough! Words contain the power of life and the power of death.

As we increase in age, we begin verbalizing our expectations about getting older. The theme seems to be centered on loss: loss of focus, independence, health, life, activity, money, etc. We absorb and speak the negative reports that tell us what to expect in each decade of life: the fifties, sixties, seventies, and so on. The media propagates these beliefs with a plethora of scary yet suggestive statistics until we fearfully internalize them. Out of the abundance of the heart, the mouth starts to express fear and dread. "I am getting old," we say and continue pledging allegiance to all of the miseries attributed to aging.

Fear attracts; Job proved this to be true in his life. Our expectations are based on hearsay, i.e., what we hear others say. We have not personally experienced whatever it is that we've heard, and yet, when we hear it, we say it too. Certainly, you know by now that the repetition of hearsay may have a hidden cost.

Unlike some, our culture has little reverence for the elderly. The focus in our culture is the young. Old age is feared, but why? One of the prevailing thoughts is that the older you become, the closer death becomes.

But exactly how old is old? Such a variance of answers was found while researching this question that it seems to depend on who is questioned. Thirty years of age is considered past prime by some sources while forty is quoted by others. Laughingly, old is deemed by some to be when a certain magazine arrives in the mail unsolicited along with an invitation to membership in this old folks' club. Age sixty-five is most agreed upon as officially old since in the past this was the age requirement for Social Security eligibility. Recent legislation may have increased the age now. You see what I mean? This precisely authenticates my point: old depends on who you ask.

How long will we continue to permit such impersonal, societal determinants such as eligibility for college, the military, marriage, Social Security, and even certain organizations determine who is old? Frankly, a number is impersonal, providing no real information about us. It determines only one fact: how long we have been on earth. Old is simply an acquisition of years: it's adding, not subtracting; increasing, not decreasing. Everyone acquires additional years, but everyone doesn't get old.

Old is a mind-set, a way of thinking. Years are not the determining factor; the real determinant is knowing God. When you know God—really know Him, not just know about Him by reading about Him—you will never grow old. How could you grow old when you have God's life inside you? We can live until we reach "biblical" old. Read your Bible to discover that people lived long lives doing phenomenal things that involved their bodies and minds. You will wonder at the number of individuals in the Bible who were centenarians yet productive mentally and physically; some even birthed children at an age we would laugh at today.

Aging is like climbing to a high floor one step at a time; it requires strength and energy. How much effort is required? How much energy is needed? How much breath was expended to reach that floor? Was there a sense of accomplishment when you arrived at the top? Was the view clearer and better? Did you realize that you must be fit to reach a high floor? That's a much better picture than what the words *age* and *years* convey. We are one with our words. Do not think or see yourself as "decrepit," "in a second childhood," an "imbecile," or "senile" though all are among the synonyms for *age* and *years*. Instead, arm yourself with loving, kind, and supportive words. See yourself as a climber. Exchange the words *age* and *years* for the word *floor*. It certainly brings to mind a more favorable visual: a floor that supports and holds up.

Don't let your beliefs or words drag you down a well-worn old path. Choose to be your best physical, mental, and emotional self. Allow *The Word Diet* recipes to help you change your words, resulting in a youthful outlook, a healthy and agile body, and a strong, competent mind.

Now get busy cooking up some longevity with the above recipes!

CHAPTER 17

Recipe for Those Desiring Marriage

Ingredients

1. Proverbs 18:2: "The man who finds a wife finds a treasure, and he receives favor from the Lord."
2. Colossians 2:10: "So you also are complete through your union with Christ, who is the head over every ruler and authority."
3. Psalm 119:165: "Those who love your instructions have great peace and do not stumble."
4. Psalm 145:16: "You open your hand and satisfy the desires of every living thing."
5. Proverbs 12:4a: "A worthy wife is a crown for her husband."
6. Proverbs 19:14: "Fathers can give their sons an inheritance of houses and wealth, but only the Lord can give an understanding wife."
7. Psalm 37:4: "Take delight in the LORD, and he will give you your heart's desires."

Preparation

Declare: The Word is working mightily in me to produce results.

The love of God assures me that I am complete in Him married or unmarried. I am the apple of God's eye. I am assured of God's love for me. I am fearfully and wonderfully made, a treasure for the man/woman God is preparing for me. I am anxiety and worry free. I rest in Him patiently knowing that there is a set time and a set mate for me. Marriage is the strong desire of my heart, thus I am victorious over my flesh. I live a godly life. I flee from sin and serve in love. I am the exceedingly great reward for my future husband/wife, a prize from God. I openly lay my desire to marry before you, Lord; nothing is hidden from you. You satisfy my heart's desires.

I am a jewel, a pious woman, loving, kind, and loyal; doing what is right and proper as best suited for me according to God's laws. I am a blessing to the man who is to be my godly mate. God said He would never forsake me, and I trust Him.

I trust the Holy Spirit, my inward witness and teacher, to lead me to a godly, pious woman who is respectful and responsive to me. She is a good woman, diligent, pious, and trustworthy. Her intent is to do me good, not evil. She will honor and uphold her marriage vows. I will cherish and protect her as my wife.

"Two heads are better than one." God is so amazing! So many expressions commonly used today come from His wisdom. There is nothing He did not think of! He established the institution of marriage between one man and one woman, so it is indeed natural to have a desire to marry. However, some may choose a single life, and that's okay for them! God allows choices, and that's their choice.

If you are desirous of marriage, I believe with you for a supernatural marriage. Set yourself in agreement with the Word of God. Vigorously stir these ingredients to enjoy a delightful result for those of you desiring marriage.

CHAPTER 18

Recipe for a Harmonious Marriage

Ingredients

1. Philippians 2:2: "Then make me truly happy by agreeing wholeheartedly with each other, loving one another, and working together with one mind and purpose."
2. 1 John 3:18: "Dear children, let's not merely say that we love each other; let us show the truth by our actions."
3. Ephesians 4:2: "Always be humble and gentle. Be patient with each other, making allowance for each other's faults because of your love."
4. Ephesians 4:3: "Make every effort to keep yourselves united in the Spirit, binding yourselves together with peace."
5. 1 Corinthians 13:7: "Love never gives up, never loses faith, is always hopeful, and endures through every circumstance."
6. 1 Corinthians 10:1: "The temptations in your life are no different from what others experience. And God is faithful. He will not allow the temptation to be more than you can stand. When you are tempted, he will show you a way out so that you can endure."
7. Mark 10:8: "...and the two are united into one. 'Since they are no longer two but one, let no one split apart what God has joined together.'"

Preparation

Declare: The Word is working mightily in me to produce results.

My wife/husband is perfect for me. We are bound together with peace. We share a love of one another as well as a love of the Lord God. We work together with one mind and purpose. Our sincere love for one another is demonstrated by our loving deeds. We are humble, not coarse or loud, each putting the needs of the other first. We walk together in love and unity under the leadership of the Holy Spirit. We endeavor to make the best of every situation that arises in our marriage. We give the enemy no place in our home.

My spouse is mine, and I am my spouse's. We are one in holy matrimony joined by God. He is in the midst of us, and we will not be moved. No one shall separate us. We do not act in opposition to God. We will not forsake our marriage. We decree that we will remain loyal to one another.

What better place to seek wisdom on marriage than from the founder of marriage, God Himself! My husband and I did not know the importance of this at the onset of our forty-two-year (and counting!) marriage. Of course, we had not submitted our lives to God at that time, and so, like any couple, we stumbled through it. We vowed of our own will that we were going to do this one time only. We had great examples in that our parents were married for a combined total of over a hundred years! They didn't set a precedent for harmony in marriage, but they certainly did a good job on the "stick-to-it-ness" of marriage. We gleaned from that, and here we are, forty-two and a half years later harmoniously married and oh so happy.

A lot of it has to do with God giving me a wonderful, low-key, and thoughtful man even before he was saved. He's gotten only better. I'm another story … But I know the Lord is not through with me. There's hope!

The Bible says that marriage makes the husband and wife become one body. Unity that carries love, respect, honor, and cooperation is the harmony equation in any marriage. The Word commands husbands to love their wives. From my perspective, that includes romance, tenderness, and thoughtfulness along with flowers, chocolates, and diamonds. Of course I'm joking; you can cancel the last three but keep the romance, tenderness, and thoughtfulness. (Smile)

Societal standards have confused the roles of a man and a wife; God, however, is not confused. Women have a role to play along with their husbands in creating a harmonious marriage. If you choose to follow biblical principles as opposed to societal standards, the role of the wife is essentially that of a helper. It says in Genesis 2:18 that God decided to make a helper for Adam. The term *helper* encompasses love, support, respect, honor, and cooperation all of which are helpful to the husband. Be sure to review time and again the recipe for a harmonious marriage.

CHAPTER 19

Recipe for Peace

Ingredients

1. Psalm 27:1: "A psalm of David. The LORD is my light and my salvation--so why should I be afraid? The LORD is my fortress, protecting me from danger, so why should I tremble?"
2. John 14:27: "I am leaving you with a gift—peace of mind and heart. And the peace I give is a gift the world cannot give. So don't be troubled or afraid."
3. Psalm 118:6: "The Lord is for me, so I will have no fear. What can mere people do to me?"
4. 2 Timothy 1:7: "For God has not given us a spirit of fear and timidity, but of power, love, and self-discipline."
5. Philippians 4:6: "Don't worry about anything; instead, pray about everything. Tell God what you need, and thank him for all he has done."
6. James 1:2: "Dear brothers and sisters, when troubles come your way, consider it an opportunity for great joy."

Preparation

Declare: The Word is working mightily in me to produce results.

Christ in me is a constant source of courage and strength. I refuse to be troubled or afraid. I count it pure joy when trouble comes my way. Troubles are an opportunity for God to show His goodness towards me. I refuse to take on the cares of the world. I have a heavenly Father who watches over me. I am in the world but not of the world, so I do not fear what the world fears. I am not fearful of sudden disaster. I do not fear bad news. I have no fear of the future. I am always in the right place at the right time with the right information and the right understanding. God orders my footsteps and shows me the way to go. I keep my mind on Him, and He keeps me in perfect peace. I trust Him. I am unshakable, profoundly assured and at peace because the Father is with me. I have hope and a future.

I am a winner. I always win. I never lose because I am blessed of the Lord. He loves me. I am a success. I am not a failure. I prosper exceedingly. I live on top, not at the bottom. I refuse to be broke, poor, or distressed. I am victorious over all circumstances. As a child of God, I cannot lose. I am of sound mind, body, and spirit. I have peace of mind and heart. I do not fear life's challenges; I meet them with power, love, and strong resolve.

The peace of knowing God is incomparable and indescribable. What troubles you? Health? Finances? The state of the world? Uncertainty of the future? Your marriage? Children? Getting old? Death? Shall I continue? No worries! In 2 Corinthians 4:8, we are told not to despair though there is trouble on every side of us.

Allow me to share an additional recipe for peace found only in the Word of God. A good place to start is Psalm 23, always a source of comfort and spiritual nourishment. It provides for all your fears; peace abides in Psalm 23. Though there are various interpretations, I am sharing what it means to me. Find your peace in this marvelous recipe and enjoy it!

	PSALM 23 Recipe for Peace
PROVISION	The Lord is my shepherd I shall not want
REST, COMFORT	He makes me to lie down in green pastures
PEACE, REST, COMFORT, QUIETNESS	He leads me beside the still waters
REDEMPTION, FORGIVENESS, STRENGTHENING	He restores my soul
RELATIONSHIP	He leads me in the path of righteousness for his name's sake
PROTECTION, TRUST, ASSURANCE	Even though I walk through the valley of the shadow of death I fear no evil, You are with me
FAITH, COMFORT	Your rod and your staff they comfort me
PROVISION, FAVOR	You prepare a table before me in the presence of my enemies
BLESSINGS, CONSECRATION	You anoint my head with oil
GOODNESS, ABUNDANCE	My cup overflows
FAVOR	Surely goodness and mercy shall follow me all the days of my life
BLESSED ASSURANCE	I will dwell in the house of the Lord forever

CHAPTER 20

Recipe for Prosperity

Ingredients

1. Job 36:11: "If they listen and obey God, they will be blessed with prosperity throughout their lives. All their years will be pleasant."
2. Luke 6:38: "Give, and you will receive. Your gift will return to you in full–pressed down, shaken together to make room for more, running over, and poured into your lap. The amount you give will determine the amount you get back."
3. Psalm 23:1: "The Lord is my shepherd; I have all that I need."
4. Malachi 3:10: "Bring all the tithes into the storehouse so there will be enough food in my Temple. If you do, says the Lord of Heaven's Armies, I will open the windows of heaven for you. I will pour out a blessing so great you won't have enough room to take it in! Try it! Put me to the test!"
5. Romans 13:8: "Owe nothing to anyone—except for your obligation to love one another. If you love your neighbor, you will fulfill the requirements of God's law."

Preparation

Declare: The Word is working mightily in me to produce results.

I am blessed. Health and wealth are in my house all the days of my life. I am wise and make wise decisions. God's wisdom demolishes scarcity in my life. I am a giver. I expect an overflowing return of whatever I give whether spiritually or materially. I lack nothing because there is no lack in God. He supplies all my needs. I am prospering in mind, body and spirit.

I am a tither. My tithing assures me of an open heaven supply that will run over me and take me over. All things are mine. I will never be broke another day in my life. Everything I touch flourishes. I am in debt to no man but for the debt of love. I am healthy in body and strong in spirit. I depend on my heavenly Father, for He gives me power to obtain wealth to fulfill His purposes. I am Abraham's descendant. The blessing of Abraham is for me, and I am walking in it. God's goodness toward me is beyond my imagination. I am living in the light of God, who directs me, and under the shield of God, who protects me. I am a recipient of all His goodness. I am growing in wisdom. I am a good steward of all that God grants me.

The church has received a plethora of abuse regarding prospering and abounding. We have been labeled the "name it and claim it" or "blab it and grab it" group. It appears that the world is offended by God's goodness to His people. However, the scriptures prove that prosperity doesn't offend God. Jesus said that He wanted us to have an abundant life (see John 10:10). He also said that He wanted us to prosper and be in good health above all else (see 3 John 1:2). God says that if our earthly fathers, who are wicked, give good gifts to their children, wouldn't He do as much, being good? (See Matthew 7:11).

The name-calling and finger-pointing is likely due in part to the world's concept of prosperity. In the natural world, prosperity equates most often to worldly goods, money in particular. The world relates to prosperity as a means of self-indulgence and self-gratification. Meanwhile, believers know for certain that without opposing financial wealth, prospering in spirit, soul, and body is a greater need. One can prosper materially yet live in a spiritually and physically weak body.

Prosperity means to fare well and to overflow. I believe everyone desires to fare well, the churched as well as the unchurched. If we have an overflowing, lovely, and godly spirit, we can also affect others. When we consider it this way, we may find prosperity more palatable. If, however, the prosperity recipes do not appeal to you, no problem! As when dining in the natural world, appetites and tastes vary.

CHAPTER 21

Recipe for Safety

Ingredients

1. Josiah 1:9: "This is my command—be strong and courageous! Do not be afraid or discouraged. For the Lord your God is with you wherever you go."
2. Isaiah 32:17: "And this righteousness will bring peace. Yes, it will bring quietness and confidence forever."
3. Proverbs 1:33: "But all who listen to me will live in peace, untroubled by fear of harm."
4. Luke 10:19: "Look, I have given you authority over all the power of the enemy, and you can walk among snakes and scorpions and crush them. Nothing will injure you."
5. Proverbs 3:24: "You can go to bed without fear; you will lie down and sleep soundly."

Preparation

Declare: The Word is working mightily in me to produce results.

I am safe regardless of what is happening in the world. God has given me His Word that it will not touch me. I walk boldly throughout every day secure in God's promises that He is

- my Protector
- my Deliverer

- my Victory
- my Strength
- my Shield
- my Dwelling Place
- my Guide
- my Light in darkness
- my Keeper
- my Restorer
- my Repairer
- my Peace
- my Blessed Assurance
- my Shepherd
- my Sanctuary
- my Hope

He is everything to the Believer. The above does not begin to tap into all that God is. Wherever I go, He is always with me. He watches over me as I sleep. I awaken safe and refreshed.

Is there any real safety on this earth? Everything we trusted as secure is now being questioned. Everything that can be shaken will be shaken as Hebrews 12:27 promises. We watch as scriptural truths unfold before our eyes on the nightly news. I don't know if today's world is any more fearful than it has been, but I know the world is full of opposition and is working diligently to make us afraid.

In this day of terrorist threats, nuclear threats, known and unknown diseases, famine, inflation, murders, financial collapse, and every type of transgression, we need the peace we can find only in God. The world takes a renewed interest in God when disasters strike, but to believers, God is our sanctuary where we dwell safely at all times. "Don't be afraid of those who want to kill your body; they cannot touch your soul. Fear only God, who can destroy both soul and body in hell" (Matthew 10:28).

The Word of God has many assurances for safety. In addition to the preceding recipe based on God's Word, I highly recommend Psalm 91. There is a peace that abides in this favorite and most popular psalm. Peace emanates from it. That peace is tangible when it is verbalized. I encourage you to memorize it and tuck it away in your heart. Please sample the recipe provided in *The Word Diet*; though it may be less familiar, it is equally as good as other recipes you know and love.

CHAPTER 22

Recipe for Strength

Ingredients

1. Mark 9:23b: "Anything is possible if a person believes."
2. Zechariah 4:6: "Then he said to me, this is what the LORD says to Zerubbabel: It is not by force nor by strength, but by my Spirit, says the LORD of Heaven's Armies."
3. Psalm 124:2: "What if the LORD had not been on our side when people attacked us?"
4. John 5:30a: "I can do nothing of my own but through the strength of my Savior I am invincible."
5. Ephesians 6:1: "A final word: Be strong in the Lord and in his mighty power."
6. Isaiah 30:15b: "This is what the Sovereign Lord, the Holy One of Israel, says: 'Only in returning to me and resting in me will you be saved. In quietness and confidence is your strength. But you would have none of it.'"

Preparation

Declare: The Word is working mightily in me to produce results.

Knowing God provides me with innumerable benefits. I am strong mentally, physically, and spiritually. There is nothing He cannot do. With God's help nothing is impossible for me. He piles on His blessings daily. They run me down and overtake me. I am blessed in the city. I am blessed in the country. I am blessed coming and going. I am blessed rising up and sitting down (Deuteronomy 28:2–6). Everything I touch prospers and grows exceedingly well. It is not by my might or power that I subdue the things that come against me; it is by His Spirit inside me. Nothing can stop me. I am strong! With God impossibility disappears for me.

I can do nothing by myself. I am not my own, but all that I am I owe to the living God—my being, movement, sight, hearing, well-being, protection, shelter, strength, and keeping. God is my friend, my confidant, my hope. For all this and much more, I thank you, Jesus! I will not complain. Where would I be if you did not love and care for me?

You, Lord, are the strength that bears me up, calms my soul, quenches my thirst, and feeds my hunger. You are the God who satisfies. You are my daily nourishment. You give me life. You give me power. You save and deliver me with your might, strength, and power. I thank you! I am confidently and quietly at peace. I draw my strength from knowing and resting in you, my deliverer. I have no trust in man but hope in you alone. In you, I am triumphant.

Strength training is an activity I engage in several times per week at a gym with my personal trainer. While I am thankful for having developed that routine early in life, there is another type of strength training I practice daily. This one is essential for the believer: confession of the Word of God. Confessions strengthen my spirit, building the muscle of faith.

You may be faced with a task that requires great strength, or you may have a life challenge pressing down on you. Developing strength, like developing muscle, requires training and consistency. Don't wait until the need is upon you; diligently train now. Develop your muscle of faith for whatever the need may be. Begin confessing *The Word Diet* recipes to help you do so.

I once experienced the loss of a loved one. We shared a very special bond. I retraced and recalled every moment we spent together during her battle with illness. I felt responsible for her loss though I had done everything I knew to do at the time. After all, I reasoned—forgetting that reasoning can be hazardous—I am the one who confesses great faith. It was only through the strength training I had developed from daily confessions that I was able to overcome. My strength muscle of faith fortified by daily confessions helped me get through that difficult time. I promise you that if you do not want to succumb to a battle, your training has to start now and be ongoing. I can say that just as confidently as I can say there will be future battles. Be ready.

Regardless of what may be looming ahead or what is crouched at our front door, there comes a time—actually, many times—when we need strength. Whatever manner of strength we are searching for—physical, mental, or spiritual—the promise from our heavenly Father is constant: "Come to me, all of you who are weary and carry heavy burdens, and I will give you rest" (Matthew 11:28). When you feel you can't go on, God's Word will provide you the pick-me-up you need. Routinely use these recipes to strengthen and develop your muscle of faith.

CHAPTER 23

Recipe for Combating Terrorism

Ingredients

1. 2 Samuel 22:3: "My God is my rock, in whom I find protection. He is my shield, the power that saves me, and my place of safety. He is my refuge, my savior, the one who saves me from violence."

2. Isaiah 54:17: "But in that coming day no weapon turned against you will succeed. You will silence every voice raised up to accuse you. These benefits are enjoyed by the servants of the Lord; their vindication will come from me. I, the Lord, have spoken!"

3. Luke 21:3: "Keep alert at all times. And pray that you might be strong enough to escape these coming horrors and stand before the Son of Man."

4. Matthew 10:28a: "Don't be afraid of those who want to kill your body; they cannot touch your soul."

5. Isaiah 54:14: "You will be secure under a government that is just and fair. Your enemies will stay far away. You will live in peace, and terror will not come near."

6. 1 Peter 1:13: "So think clearly and exercise self-control. Look forward to the gracious salvation that will come to you when Jesus Christ is revealed to the world."

7. Jeremiah 32:21: "You brought Israel out of Egypt with mighty signs and wonders, with a strong hand and powerful arm, and with overwhelming terror."

Preparation

Declare: The Word is working mightily in me to produce results.

Lord, you are my shield, my protector, and refuge. I hide in you. You save me from violence. No weapon whether physical, spiritual, or verbal can hurt me because you are my Vindicator. I am aware of the times and their significance; I keep alert always. I will not be tempted to fall away from my faith. I am not fearful of man, who cannot touch my soul. I fear you only. I live in peace. Terror will not touch me.

I recognize the world's seduction and desire no part in it. I refuse to depart from the faith. God, you have proven that you will deliver your people as you have done before. You will avenge all wrongs, you said. I believe it. It is so. I do not return evil for evil; I trust you, God, to keep me.

There is a distinct fear invading today's world, a fear that until recently Americans have not encountered—the fear of terrorism. During my preparation for this material, I discovered that the U.S. government agencies who work to defeat terrorism have no single definition of what terrorism is. That seems a bit incongruous. However, the one commonality upon which they all agree is that terrorism encompasses some form of violence. Violence evokes trepidation, and this is precisely fear's purpose. Naturally, the world's response to terror is fear. Fear is effectively working in the world right now. It is running rampant throughout the world today.

Fear is a spirit (see 2 Timothy. 1:7). Terrorism has heightened the ever-increasing level of dread globally, and fear is swiftly becoming the way of the world. The world seems to dwell in fear as a rule. You can prove it by turning on any form of media. Listen to the voices of the world and tell me what you hear. We are holding ourselves in terror.

Nevertheless, the church should not be startled. Consider John 16:2–3, which so aptly asserts, "The time is coming when those who kill you will think they are doing a holy service for God. This is because they have never known the Father or me. Yes, I'm telling you these things now, so that when they happen, you will remember my warning." Despite what's going on around us, the church must hold onto faith in God and not abandon it in fear.

Let your light shine! This is our opportunity to stand out and be witnesses for God as God has called us to be. There are but two choices—faith or fear—and the response of the church must be faith. This recipe combines a mixture of faith and spiritual resolve in an effort to defeat the fear you may personally experience when you hear news about terror of any sort.

CHAPTER 24

Recipe for Weight Control

Ingredients

1. Philippians 3:19: "Their god is their appetite, they brag about shameful things, and they think only about this life here on earth."
2. 1 Corinthians 9:27: "I discipline my body like an athlete, training it to do what it should."
3. Proverbs 25:28: "A person without self-control is like a city with broken-down walls."
4. 1 Corinthians 6:20: "For God bought you with a high price. So you must honor God with your body."
5. Matthew 6:25b: "Isn't life more than food, and your body more than clothing?"

Preparation

Declare: The Word is working mightily in me to produce results.

My body celebrates God. I refuse to allow my body to rule over me. The greater One lives in me. I exercise control over fleshly desires; I declare myself free from the lust of food. I tell my body what to do. My body does not tell me what to do; I am free from the reign of flesh. I will not yield to the temptation of overindulgent eating. Life is more than food to me. I refuse thoughts of food and eat only for nourishment. I refuse all unhealthy snacks. I cast down thoughts of chips, pop, sugary foods, buttery foods, and all foods that may be injurious to my weight control plan. In Jesus's name!

Sensual pleasures such as food are not my god, for I will not allow my body to rule over me. I discipline my body like an athlete. I train my body to restrain from overindulgent activities like eating too much. I turn to the Lord to keep me safe from the battle of overeating being waged against me. The Lord gives me power and strength to fight gastronomic temptations. I give myself bodily and fully to God, a living holy sacrifice. God bought me for a high price, and I will not eat more than I need. I will keep my body healthy. I will honor the high price God paid for me.

Although the Word Diet is a book about word weight, I could not resist the temptation to include a bit about natural weight loss at the end. Do not be surprised to discover that weight control is discussed in the Word of God; there is nothing new under the sun. Though you will not find the phrase *weight control* used explicitly in the Word of God, you will see the term *gluttony* used on several occasions. Gluttony is mostly associated with overeating but can be applied to overindulgence of any type. It is an archaic word not much used anymore; consequently, our culture—even within Christianity—is likely unfamiliar with it.

According to Wikipedia, *gluttony* means overindulgence or overconsumption of food, drink, or anything to the point of extravagance or waste.[8]

Realizing that we all love food, the subject of overeating is unpopular and we are hesitant to bring it up. Yet God calls repeated overindulgence of any type gluttony. I believe this to be the reason it is mentioned in the scriptures. Gluttony is viewed as a lack of self-control or self-discipline. I do not feel that gluttony is mentioned in the Bible to focus on *overeating* as much as the sins that overindulgence or lack of discipline can lead to in other areas. To lead a godly life, we must control our flesh. Believers need to know that failing to discipline our physical desires is giving free rein to our flesh in other areas. It is a door left open for the entrance of many fleshy temptations, anything—not just eating—done in excess is gluttony.

Of course, not all obesity is a result of overeating; however, overeating

---

[8] "seven deadly sins," Wikipedia.com, http://en.wikipedia.org/wiki/seven_deadly_ sins#Gluttony.

is regularly associated with gluttony. It is difficult to admit to any type of weakness; we do not like this picture of ourselves and often see it as a failure. I believe this to be a deception fed to us by the enemy causing us to take no action. Some Christians consider gluttony a sin, but in this world of overindulgence, it appears that this line of thought is passé. Christians are proud to say the following phrase from an old rhyme from the nineteenth century: "I don't smoke, and I don't chew, and I don't go with girls who do."[9] Yes, drinking and smoking can be injurious and can lead to ruin. Yet as a whole, Christians neglect overeating, which can be just as harmful.

We are bombarded with food suggestions all around us; on nearly every corner in the United States is some type of eating establishment. That in addition to the fact that food can be so deliciously satisfying makes it difficult not to yield to the temptation of eating more than we need. Even when we have recently eaten, we can still be enticed to take just one more bite, have a little dessert, or taste a small morsel of food that we long to sample.

The fact that eating establishments offer enormous serving sizes only adds to the temptation to overeat. A generous serving increases the likelihood that we will eat all of it; psychologically, we feel better about doing so. And leaving food on the plate is regarded as a no-no by some and may be regarded as an insult in some cultures. I have heard some say that it is a sin to leave food on the plate because it is considered waste.

If you struggle with weight control, the recipes provided in addition to a few other tips can help you get your weight under control.

1. **Order and share a single serving with a companion.**
   This is a practice my husband and I have adopted when dining out. Splitting one serving and putting it on two plates helps limit the amount eaten and eliminates waste. This practice allows you to eat the entire meal but a smaller portion.

2. **Ask for a carryout container.**

---

[9] Tim.

Don't feel obligated to clean your plate. Don't feel it is wasteful when you can't eat an entire portion. Remember, restaurants are in the business of serving much-too-large portions to keep you coming back!

3. **Just say no to excessive food.**

   Just say no was an advertising campaign prevalent during the 1980s and early 1990s to discourage children from engaging in drugs. The slogan became popular and expanded to other venues. Though I am unsure how effective it was in the battle against drugs, I do know that a no said with meaning and force is a little word with big power!

   The word *no* is a form of resistance, in this case spoken resistance. We can just say no to excessive food consumption. Believers can just say no to the many temptations of the world: "So humble yourselves before God. Resist the devil and he will flee from you" (James 4:7). Ask the Holy Spirit to help you. Consider fasting as another good way to tame the flesh.

We are spiritual beings, and God has given us dominion over all things on earth; our bodies are on the earth, and thus food is on the earth. Take dominion over your body and over food. Speak to your body: "No, you will not eat that!" "No, you will not do that." Adopt this position and speak it: "I tell my body what to do; my body does not tell me what to do."

The weight control recipes contained herein may not refer directly to overeating, but they are helpful in the battle to control our appetites. The recipes are also another way to just say no. God has blessed us by filling the earth with foods that are delicious, nutritious, and pleasurable. We should honor God's creation by enjoying these foods and by eating them in appropriate quantities. Plant the Word of God in your heart and expect a sweet harvest. WOW the world by **W**inning **O**ver **W**eight!

CHAPTER 25

Spiritual Smoothie

Do you need some nourishment to get you going in the morning? Delight in a spiritual smoothie. This smoothie is invigorating and contains life-giving properties that will nourish your spirit, soul, and body. The spiritual smoothie quenches your thirst as you drink from the fountain of God. Smoothies have become a morning ritual for many. Some people, dieters and non-dieters both, use smoothies as a meal replacement that keeps them going until the next meal. Depending on what ingredients you add to them, they may also have some health benefits. Smoothies typically consist of a variety of ingredients in delightful combinations including but not limited to fruits, vegetables, yogurt, supplemental powders, ice, water, milk, and a host of other alternatives.

Though this smoothie is spiritual, it too consists of a variety of ingredients, but is based on one source, the Word of God. It covers but is not limited to health, wealth, well-being and a host of other things. The confessions may be delightfully combined to meet your particular taste. Savor this spiritual smoothie every morning by allowing God to pour out His spirit into yours. It is certainly a great way to begin your day! Let the robust mixture of God's Word saturate your palate. This smoothie will last long past breakfast as God's Word is eternal! Warning—it can be addictive; it's just that good. I encourage you to drink from this spiritual smoothie every morning and watch God perform a change on the inside of you with every sip. He did it for me!

Spiritual Smoothie

- Now that I am born again, I have a new understanding of who I really am.
- I am a spirit being.
- I am in the world but not of the world.
- I am created to make a difference in this world.
- I set the course of my life today with my words.
- My words have life and death power (Proverbs 18:21).
- I am a winner.
- I always win; I never lose.
- God gives me grace to excel in all that I do (2 Corinthians 8:7).
- All things are mine.
- I am successful.
- I refuse to struggle.
- I refuse to fear.
- I am invincible, undefeatable, and special.
- Whatever I do thrives.
- God gives me the true riches of the world.
- Prosperity has overtaken me.
- I refuse poverty.
- I will never be broke another day in my life.
- Wealth and riches are in my house (Psalm 112:3).
- I am sound in body, mind, and spirit.
- I walk in love.
- I am kind, compassionate, and just with others.
- I refuse to be held captive by sickness, disease, or pain.
- I will never be sick another day in my life.
- I have a sound mind. I retain what I need to retain.
- I have a surplus of energy.
- I am the best.
- I am in right relationship with God, being counted as righteous.
- In the name of Jesus, I decree that this is my set time to prosper. This is my set time to be whole. What I believe is what I automatically become, and I believe your Word. Father, I pray that you cause me to see the reality of your power as recorded in your Word.

- Thank you, Lord. Today is the best day of my life!

As you continue to speak the Word aloud, faith will enter your heart and develop the strength to carry you through your day. This is among my favorite smoothie recipes! It is my daily tonic. Be mindful that your faith—the contents of what you desire to manifest—will develop over time through repetition.

Position yourself to routinely read, study, meditate and hear the Word of God and faith will surely come. Like a path is worn in the dirt by walking over it repeatedly, the repetitiveness of speaking the Word from your mouth will build a route of faith for everything declared out of your mouth. If you set time aside to confess God's Word, your life will change dramatically. Knowing there are limitless benefits and magnanimous results, it is beyond imagination why believers do not invest more time with the God they claim to love. If perhaps you are unable to fit a super-sized spiritual smoothie into your schedule, consider taking smaller sips to quench your thirst throughout the day. Enjoy!

CHAPTER 26

A Call to Action

Create Your Own Word Diet Recipes

God's Word is a book of delicacies for the believer. You need more than natural food to live this life in victory. Eat from it with no fear of overindulgence or weight gain. The recipes in *The Word Diet* do not claim to be comprehensive. You may have needs not addressed here. However, God knows your needs, and you can be sure He won't neglect them. If you were unable to find a recipe that satisfies your needs, now that you have sampled those in *The Word Diet*, create recipes that do! Every good cook knows how to plan a savory and satisfying meal. It is common practice for great cooks to boast about their culinary skills. Though each may have similar recipes for the same dish, they add their own special touches, tweaking it just a bit to suit their palates and make the dish unique. Create your own recipes using His Word as a food source.

To create a spiritual recipe for your personal need(s), you too can choose a host of healthy, life-sustaining, and faith-maintaining ingredients from the Word of God.

1. Locate a scripture that addresses your need directly or indirectly.
2. Meditate on the scripture.
3. Trust the Holy Spirit for revelation.
4. Make God's Word your word. Personalize it!
5. Begin to confidently speak the Word aloud as frequently as you desire. Garnish with a lot of praise and thank-you.
6. Rejoice in the manifestation for it will surely come.

God's Word is full of recipes for life. The best way to uncover these delightful recipes is by delving faith first into His Word. *The Word Diet* works if you work it!

Get hungry, but stick to a diet regimen of the Word. I invite you to come, sit, and sup at the heavenly banquet of God, which is all you can eat! "There is nothing better than to enjoy food and drink and to find satisfaction in work" (Ecclesiastes 2:24).

As you learn to cook with the Book, prepare your palate to enjoy meals from *The Word Diet*.

Before You Close the Book

Everyone loves good food. I invite you to partake of the best food you will ever eat. All are invited to dine. "The Lord isn't really being slow about his promise, as some people think. No, he is being patient for your sake. He does not want anyone to be destroyed, but wants everyone to repent." (2 Peter 3:9) There is one requirement however, you must have a meal ticket. The meal ticket that you will need to eat at God's table is based on Romans 10:9. "If you confess with your mouth that Jesus is Lord and believe in your heart that God raised Him from the dead, you will be saved."

Action steps:

1. Repent of your sins.
2. Declare Jesus to be Lord of your life.
3. Believe.
4. Receive

Repeat this prayer with heartfelt sincerity.

Dear Heavenly Father,
I repent of my sins. Forgive me.
I declare with my mouth that," Jesus is Lord."
I believe in my heart that God raised Jesus from the dead.
I receive Jesus as my Lord and Savior.
Thank You Father for saving me!

Theresa Byrd-Smith, first-time author, appropriately hits the ground running with her premier book, *The Word Diet*. Theresa is a longtime fitness enthusiast who believes that it is the custodial duty of the soul who inhabits this earthly temple to care for it, keeping the mind, body, spirit, and soul at an optimum level.

Due to her activity level and weight dominance, she is routinely queried about her accomplishments in these areas. Initially, she began sharing tips with a short-lived blog that evolved into *The Word Diet*. In *The Word Diet*, Theresa shares a fascinating look at the connection of our words with our weight. She introduces a concept she calls "word weight." She confirms the connection with the Word of God. Theresa, a former educator and school administrator for both private and public schools is uniquely positioned and appropriately qualified to teach. She is passionate about teaching and is led by Psalm 51:13 (NKJV): "Then will I teach transgressors your ways; and sinners shall be converted unto you." Having spent a lifetime in various pedagogical roles, it is only befitting that she assumes the role of teacher once again in her debut book, *The Word Diet*.

Theresa is a runner who has completed a half-marathon plus numerous 5 and 10 k runs. She is a longtime member of Living Word Christian Center, she completed Foundation classes and studied at the Living Word Bible Training Center in Forest Park, Illinois. Theresa earned a Master of Arts degree from Roosevelt University in Chicago and a Bachelor of Arts degree from Fisk University in Nashville, Tennessee. She is a Toastmasters International Competent Communicator, Competent Leader and Competent Toastmaster serving currently as a local club president. She has won numerous recognitions for her speaking gift. She is also a member of the Global Christian Professional Women's Association. She and her husband, James, reside in a Chicago suburb.

You may contact Theresa at byrdsmith07@att.net for your next speaking event.

WORKS CITED

"adult obesity facts." www.cdc.gov/obesity/data/adult.html (accessed 22 September 2016).

"list of diets." Wikipedia.com, https://en.wikipedia.org/wiki/List_of_diets (accessed 26 September 2016).

"seven deadly sins." Wikipedia.com, http://en.wikipedia.org/wiki/seven_deadly_sins#Gluttony (accessed 12 October 2016).

"talk." Dictionary.com, http://www.dictionary.com/browse/talk (accessed 17 December 2015).

"weight." Merriam Webster.com, http://www.merriam-webster.com (accessed 12 January 2016).

Rasbeary, Dr. James. http://broraz.com/2012/04/17/article_the_sheep_and_the_anointing_oil (accessed 17 May 2016).

Sharpe, Lindsey. *U.S. Obesity Rate Climbing in 2013*, http://www.gallup.com. (accessed 12 May 2016).

Stewart, Tim. *Dictionary of Christianese, Casual Slang of the Christian Church... Authoritativrly Defined* http://www.dictionaryofchristianese.com (accessed 4 October 2016).

Tennyson, Ros. *Betwixt & Between*, http://partnershipbrokers.org/w/journal choosing ourwordswithcare/ (accessed 12 May 2016).

Printed in the United States
By Bookmasters